AROUND THE WORLD IN A HUNDRED YEARS

FROM HENRY THE NAVIGATOR TO MAGELLAN

Jean Fritz

Illustrated by Anthony Bacon Venti

The Putnam & Grosset Group

To

Mika and Charlotte

who live where the explorers

wanted to go.

With gratitude to John Noble Wilford
for his careful reading of the manuscript.

Text copyright © 1994 by Jean Fritz.
Illustrations copyright © 1994 by Anthony Bacon Venti.
All rights reserved. This book, or parts thereof, may not be reproduced
in any form without permission in writing from the publisher.
A PaperStar Book, published in 1998 by The Putnam & Grosset Group,
200 Madison Avenue, New York, NY 10016.
PaperStar is a registered trademark of The Putnam Berkley Group, Inc.
The PaperStar logo is a trademark of The Putnam Berkley Group, Inc.
Originally published in 1994 by G. P. Putnam's Sons.
Published simultaneously in Canada
Printed in Hong Kong
Book designed by Nanette Stevenson and Donna Mark.
Text is set in Sabon.

Library of Congress Cataloging-in-Publication Data
Fritz, Jean. Around the world in a hundred years: Henry the Navigator to
Magellan / Jean Fritz; illustrated by Anthony Bacon Venti. p. cm.
Includes bibliographical references and index.
Summary: Examines the great wave of European exploration
during the fifteenth century which resulted in more accurate maps.
1. Explorers—Juvenile literature. 2. Discoveries in geography—Juvenile
literature. [1. Explorers. 2. Discoveries in geography.] I. Venti, Anthony Bacon, ill.
II. Title. G175.F75 1993 910′.92′2—dc20 92-27042 CIP AC
ISBN 0-698-11638-0

10 9 8 7 6 5 4

Contents

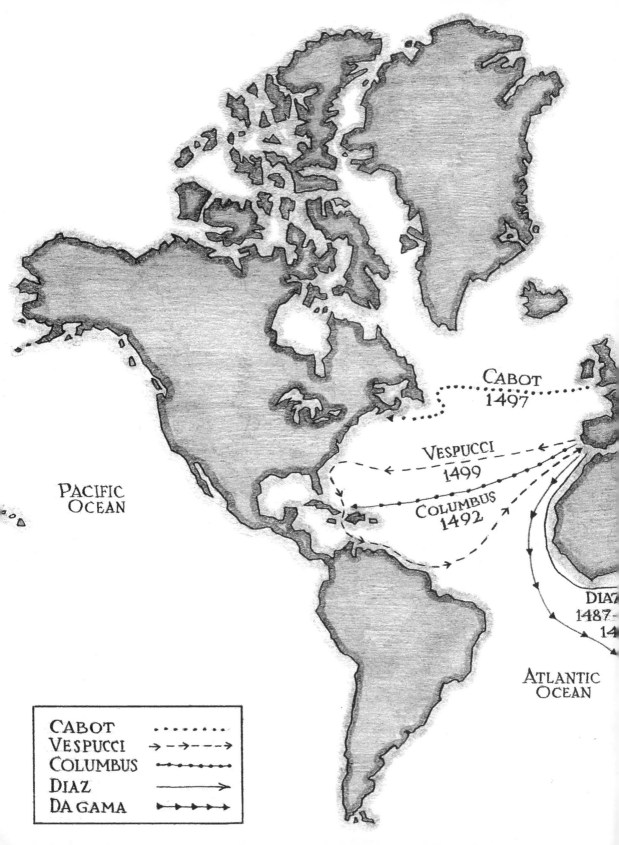

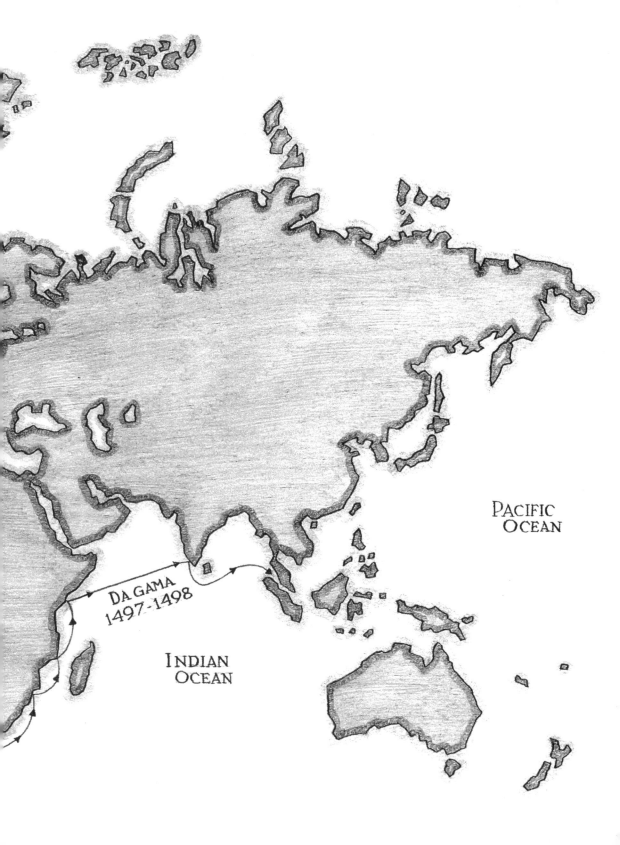

PACIFIC
OCEAN

DA GAMA
1497-1498

INDIAN
OCEAN

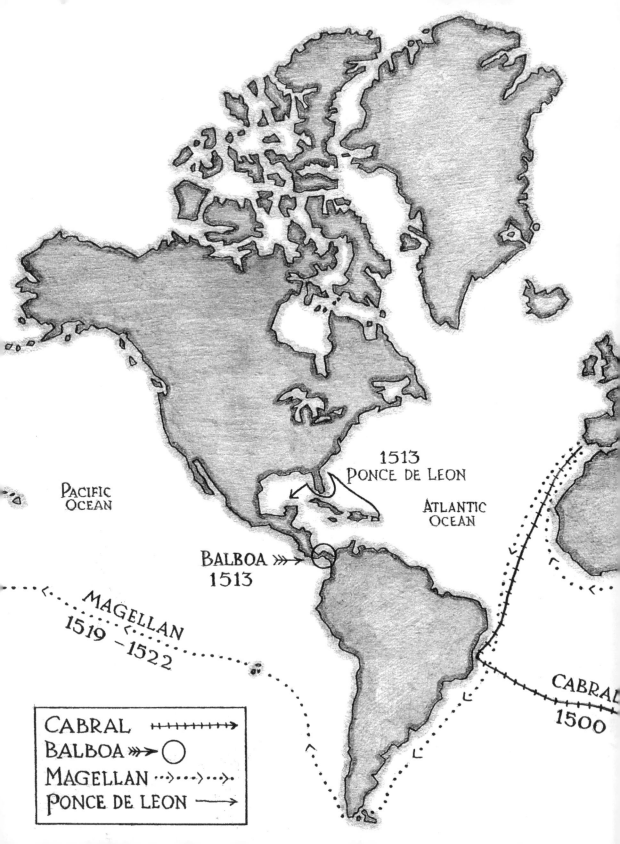

1513
PONCE DE LEON

PACIFIC
OCEAN

ATLANTIC
OCEAN

BALBOA »»»
1513

MAGELLAN
1519 –1522

CABRAL
1500

CABRAL ++++++++++→
BALBOA »»»→ ○
MAGELLAN ··>·>·>·>·
PONCE DE LEON ——→

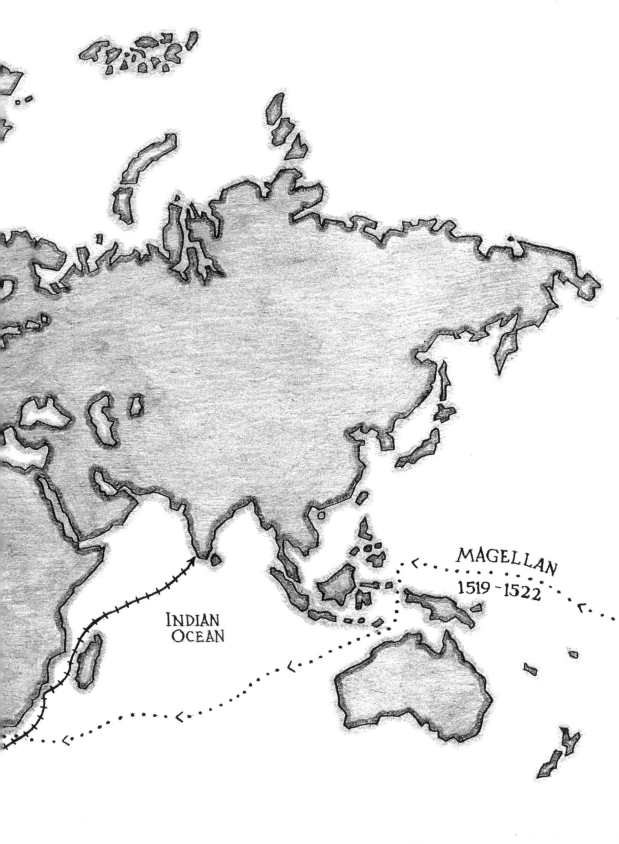

INDIAN
OCEAN

MAGELLAN
1519 - 1522

I

Before the Explorers

IF YOU WERE TO LOOK AT A MAP of the world as it appeared to people in Europe six hundred or more years ago in the fourteenth century, you would wonder how mapmakers could have been so mixed up. There was Asia, for instance, ending up in a curly tail pointing at Africa. Asia, of course, was far away from Europe, but Africa was right next door and mapmakers didn't know how to finish it off. Either they let the whole continent dribble away to nothing or they made up any old shape that they pleased. They also added an imaginary continent that stretched across the bottom of most maps. Why? For balance, they said. It was only logical. Otherwise the world would be top-heavy. Finally, there was empty space at the edge of every map which everyone knew was the Unknown.

So why didn't someone go out and take a look?

A mapmaker in 1400 would have told you that the map showed all there was to the world. There was no more. Besides, people knew all they needed to know. It was common knowledge that the Unknown sucked you under. Or burned you up. Or simply left you to rot in nowhere. No one who tried to go there could possibly get back. No one wanted to go and no one was curious.

But in earlier times people had been curious and philosophers had tried to figure out what the world was like. Aristotle, for instance, who lived in the fourth century B.C., noticed that the shadow of the earth on the moon during an eclipse was curved. That meant that the earth was a sphere, he said. The sun and moon must revolve around it. Other philosophers agreed. Claudius Ptolemy, who lived four hundred years later in the second century after Christ, and is called the Father of Geography, placed north at the top of the map and east at the right-hand side. He applied astronomy and mathematics to the study of the earth and experimented in drawing the sphere upon the flat surface of a map, allowing for the curve of the earth. He divided the sphere into grids of latitude and longitude, which were supposed to make it easier for navigators to know where they were. The latitude represents an imaginary line parallel to the equator. Every degree is equal to about sixty-nine miles either north or south of the equator.

In addition, navigators had compasses and crude instruments to help them fix their position by observing the angle of the sun or of the North Star. No instrument had been invented yet to determine the longitude, the north-south lines on a map which established the distance as one traveled from east to west or west to east. There was no clock that kept accurate time on a rolling ocean. All anyone could do was to guess at the speed of the boat, but since this was not an accurate measurement,

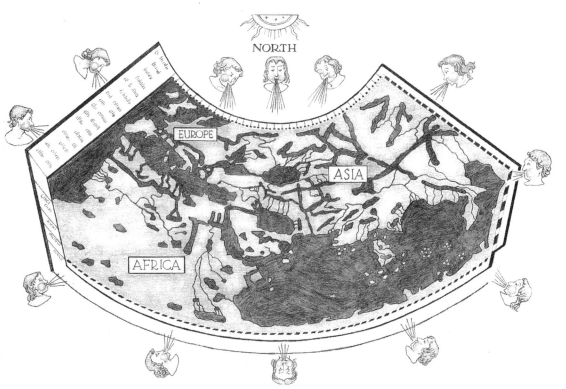

PTOLEMY'S MAP

many of Ptolemy's calculations were wrong. He estimated, for instance, that the circumference of the earth was 18,000 miles, about three-fourths its actual size, and he put the equator 400 miles too far north. Still, he did try to make a systematic picture of the world based on scientific principles, and he identified eight thousand places.

Then suddenly all this wondering and figuring stopped. Christianity was a new religion, fighting for survival, and in A.D. 391 Christians burned the city of Alexandria and its famous libraries, which contained, along with many ancient treasures of scholarship, the work of Ptolemy. Christians did not believe in scholarship. They thought it was sacrilegious to be curious. Anything people wanted to know, they said, could be found in the Bible. So when they drew maps, they put Jerusalem at the center of the world. East was on the top of the map with the Garden of Eden sprawled across it, and according to some people, the world was flat. Didn't the Bible talk of the "four corners" of the earth? Anything with corners was square and flat. World maps at this time

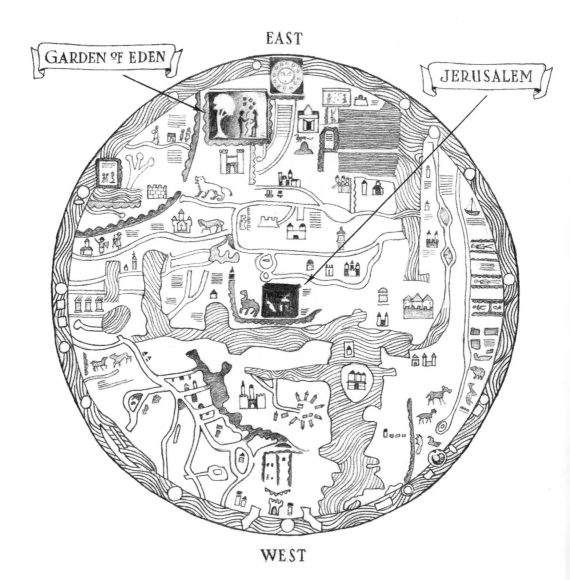

EAST

GARDEN OF EDEN

JERUSALEM

WEST

were largely decorative. They were not meant to be guides to help people get around, but pictures to prove the glory of God. And in order to make the sea more interesting, mapmakers scattered islands around—some legendary, some with made-up names, some with no names.

Europeans went on thinking like this for over one thousand years, but in China there were already fairly accurate maps of that part of the world. Some of these maps included such distant places as the Nile River, Sudan, Zanzibar, and part of the Mediterranean Sea. Of course the Chinese knew nothing about the Atlantic Ocean and what lay beyond, but in 1405, before Europeans had begun sending out explorers, a Chinese navigator, Chêng Ho, was leading expeditions of 317 ships and 37,000 men to nearly every land bordering the China Sea and the Indian Ocean. The largest of these ships carried nine masts and was 444 feet long, which, of course, would have astounded Christopher Columbus, whose *Santa María* measured somewhere between 75 and 90 feet. In a total of seven expeditions Chêng Ho took these ships as far west as the entrance of the Persian Gulf and the mouth of the Red Sea. In 1433, however, a new emperor decided that all this traipsing around to different countries was a waste of time. After all, he said, China was the center of the world; it had everything that it needed or wanted. So the Chinese stayed home.

Although Europeans would not have seen Chêng Ho's fabulous flotilla, they may have heard rumors of it. If so, these stories only emphasized again what Europeans already knew. China, and indeed the entire Indies, was an exotic place. Hadn't Marco Polo, that young Venetian who had crossed deserts and mountains to reach China, written a firsthand account of the splendor and riches he had seen during his seventeen years there? Many people didn't believe his fantastic tales; still, they couldn't forget them. Besides, he had brought back

rubies and emeralds and diamonds which people could see with their own eyes. Other travelers, missionaries and traders, also had stories of precious stones, spices, and silks that could be found throughout the Indies. So Europeans built up a picture of what a marvelous place the Indies must be. It was too bad it was so hard to get there.

About the same time as the Chinese were stopping their overseas ventures, Europe was waking up. Beginning in the fourteenth century, change began creeping over the continent. For one thing, more people had traveled. There had always been traders and missionaries, and even ordinary people sometimes made pilgrimages to holy places—to Rome, if they could manage it, and even to Jerusalem, their Holy City. Although Jerusalem had been in the hands of the Muslims since 637, Christians were treated well when they came on pilgrimages. But in the eleventh century the ruling Muslims began to harass visiting Christians and to molest their shrines. So now all Europe was up in arms. In a fever of enthusiasm they set out to rescue Jerusalem. Men, women, and children—many who had never been away from home before—rich and poor together streamed across Europe to the Holy Land. Because they carried crosses, they were called crusaders. Between 1095 and 1271, there were nine crusades. Although the crusaders did manage to recapture Jerusalem on the First Crusade, they lost it again and were never able to take it back on any of their later expeditions. Still, when the crusaders returned home, they were not the same people. They had seen so many new places, met so many new people, and encountered so many new experiences that, although they were as religious as ever, they had, almost without knowing it, made room in their minds for new ideas.

And new ideas were coming. By 1406 a copy of Ptolemy's *Geography* had been rediscovered and translated into Latin, and Ptolemy quickly became the authority on all geographical questions. No one doubted

now that the earth was a sphere. Interest was revived in other ancient Greek and Latin writers. And in the first half of the fifteenth century Johann Gutenberg invented movable type, and as books were printed, more people read. They became more curious and asked questions.

Moreover, people in Spain and the countries along the Atlantic seaboard were feeling hemmed in by the Muslim world which almost surrounded them. They felt threatened by people who had a different religion and different customs. And they resented the fact that Muslims controlled the spice market in the Indies. Europeans needed spices, particularly cloves, which not only helped to preserve meat but covered up the taste when it was spoiled. They were big meat-eaters, but the only way they could get spices was to buy them from traders who went to Egypt and other Muslim countries. But not every trader could even get there. Two Italian cities, Venice and Genoa, took charge of the Mediterranean Sea. If people wanted spices, they had to buy them from Venetian and Genoese traders. And who could afford the prices that the Venetians and Genoese charged? Raised five hundred times their price, spices became so valuable, they were often used instead of money. The only other route to the spices, silks, and gold of the Indies was by caravan from Constantinople across the long overland road to China. This is the route that Marco Polo took, but the round trip took three years and goods obtained this way were also expensive. By 1453 even this route would be cut off when the Turks, at war with Christians, took the city of Constantinople and refused to allow any overland travel.

So now there was not only an interest in the geography of the world but a need to know more about it.

It was time to take a look at the Unknown.

COAST
OF
AFRICA

SPAIN

PORTUGAL

EXPLORATION OF THE
AFRICAN COAST

1421

1460

2

Prince Henry the Navigator

WAS THE UNKNOWN COMPLETELY UNKNOWN?

Today everyone knows that the Vikings in northern Europe once built a settlement on land across the ocean in what would become known as the New World, but at the time people in Europe probably didn't hear about it. If they had, they would not have been impressed. Those Vikings! they would have said. They had always done outrageous things. What if they *had* found land? It couldn't have been worth much or they would have gone back.

There were also stories of ships being driven by storms into unknown waters, perhaps even onto unknown shores. But no one paid attention. An accident to an unimportant sailor, no matter what tale he told, was not news. People in Europe had decided what the world was like, and it would take more than a few lost sailors to change their minds.

What it took was just one man, Prince Henry of Portugal. He became obsessed with that mysterious African coastline which the mapmakers had never been able to finish. Born on March 4, 1394, the third son of King John of Good Memory, Henry might well have followed the unquestioning ideas of his father and his father's generation. He was certainly religious enough, but the Bible alone could not answer the questions he asked when he looked out from the shores of Portugal at the wilderness of water before him. Particularly interested in the study of mathematics and astronomy, Prince Henry learned early that the best way to solve a problem was to go at it slowly, deliberately, one step at a time. He took his first step when he was twenty-five years old and built himself a modest house on the southern tip of Portugal, where he could stand with Europe at his back, Africa before him, and the Unknown crashing against the boundaries in between.

Although Henry was fiercely curious by nature, his curiosity about Africa had been fired when at the age of twenty-one he led an expedition against the Moorish (Muslim) city of Ceuta in Morocco, directly across the Mediterranean Sea from Gibraltar. Christians never forgot that they wanted to make the whole world Christian, so of course they considered any war against the Muslims a Holy War and anyone who led it was a hero. Prince Henry certainly looked a hero, dressed in fancy new clothes, as were all the members of his gilded seventy-ship fleet. From the northern port of Pôrto (or Oporto) they sailed in formation— the smallest ships first, then the big ships, then the galleys and Prince Henry in his own galley at the rear. Ceuta was not an easy city to conquer, but conquer it they did, and then as victors, they took the spoils. And what spoils there were! It was as if these Portuguese were ransacking the Indies, for the city was filled with Eastern treasures—

silver, gold, Persian carpets, Indian muslins, and sacks of cinnamon, pepper, cloves, and ginger brought to Ceuta by the Muslims on their secret trade route through the Red Sea.

Although the Muslim trade stopped at Ceuta as soon as Christians took over, Prince Henry stayed long enough to hear about places unknown to Europeans, including the east coast of Africa, which the Muslims knew well. But the west coast? No, they didn't know the west coast. The sea was not navigable there, he was told. Muslims called it the Green Sea of Darkness. It was the same old story that Henry had always heard. Just what Christians said. Everyone seemed to agree that if you went down the west coast of Africa, you would come to a point where the water boiled, where people turned black, where ships caught fire, where the air itself was poisonous.

But how could you be sure? Henry asked. Had anyone seen the water boil? He determined to provide ships and finance anyone who would go and find some of the answers. So when John Gonçalves and Tristan Vaz, two young men who had fought with him at Ceuta, asked him for jobs, Prince Henry gave them the command of two ships and told them to sail down the coast of Africa. Go as far as you can, he said. Keep records of all you see. Bring back specimens of plants.

They didn't get far. They were still off the coast of Morocco when a storm drove them so far out to sea, they were afraid they had been blown into dragon territory. But when the storm was over, there they were beside a small, green island. They knew that some islands, like the Canary Islands, had already been discovered, but this looked like a brand-new undiscovered island, and since there were no people around, it didn't even need to be conquered. All it needed was a name, so they called it Porto Santo, grabbed some plant specimens, and three days later rushed back to Portugal to tell Prince Henry the good news.

Prince Henry was always interested in empty islands. If they were colonized, they could serve as way stations for the explorers he planned to recruit. So he sent Gonçalves and Vaz back to Porto Santo with supplies, a few settlers, seeds, plants, and also a third partner for their venture, a man named Bartholomew Perestrelo. At the last minute Bartholomew took a pregnant rabbit on board, and off they sailed. As it turned out, the seeds and plants flourished. But so did the rabbits. At the end of two years there were so many rabbits, they took over the island. Bold and brazen, they acted as if the crops had been planted just for them. No matter how many rabbits the men shot, there were

always more, armies on the munch, stripping away the fields. In the end, the men gave up. They left the island to the rabbits and returned to Portugal.

Prince Henry told Gonçalves and Vaz to find another island. And they did. When they had been in Porto Santo, they had seen something in the south which they thought might be an island, so they went back and, sure enough, it was. They sailed home and reported the new find to Prince Henry, who sent them out again with seeds, plants, and more men. Gonçalves also took his wife, his twelve-year-old son, and his two little daughters. They called this island Madeira (which means "wood"), and in time the two islands, along with neighboring small, undeveloped islands, became known as the Madeira Islands. The trouble on this island was not rabbits, but trees. They were so thick and the undergrowth was so heavy that the men had trouble clearing any land. Why not burn off some of those trees, Gonçalves suggested.

So they set one section of the woods on fire. Once it started, however, the fire couldn't be stopped. It roared out of control until the entire island was in flames. The people fled to their boats and sailed to Portugal for help. All but Gonçalves and his wife and children. They stayed on the beach in a makeshift shelter and when the wind blew smoke and sparks too close, they climbed onto rocks or waded into the water. They couldn't step on dry land for two days, yet while waiting for help, they managed to feed themselves on birds and fish. When help arrived, the fire was still raging in one valley and continued to smolder for seven years, but the colonists went ahead in other parts of the island and planted on top of the ashes. Plant grapes, Prince Henry told them. Grapes should do well on a bed of ashes, and they did. The wine from those grapes, known as Madeira, has been famous ever since.

As for Bartholomew Perestrelo, Prince Henry made him governor of Porto Santo. He returned, but instead of planting crops this time, he

~BÁRCA~

~CARAVEL~

raised cattle. Apparently, the rabbits were in good health because people thirty years later still talked about them.

Meanwhile, Prince Henry was gathering charts, building ships, learning everything he could about sailing. He invited Master Jaime, the most famous geographer in Europe, to join him at his headquarters. Astronomers, cartographers, sea captains—all came to exchange information and discuss the secrets of the sea. First they had to decide what kind of ship to use. Certainly not the *barca,* the square-rigged trading ship most frequently seen lumbering through the Mediterranean Sea. For exploring down the African coastline, they would need something smaller and easier to manage, one that could sail against the wind as well as with the wind. Of course there was no point in sending a ship into unknown waters if it couldn't get back. So they chose a *caravel,* adapting and improving the design of ancient Arab ships and incorporating features of the little *caravela,* which skimmed through Portuguese rivers. A caravel had three triangular sails instead of two square-rigged ones and it was only about seventy feet long (with room for approximately twenty men and their supplies.) Most important, it could turn into the wind and come home.

The trouble was that Prince Henry's ships kept coming home too soon. They could never seem to get beyond Cape Bojador, that bulge on the African coast just south of the Canary Islands where the boiling water was supposed to begin. From 1421 to 1433, one after another, his ships went down the coast, but even as they approached Cape Bojador, the sailors could hear the pounding surf. They could sense the demons that were driving the fierce wind, ploughing up the ocean, sweeping up yellow storms of sand to blind and confound them. And beyond? They shuddered at what lay ahead. So again and again they turned back.

Prince Henry was patient. Don't be scared by old tales, he said. Go a little farther this time.

In 1434 Gil Eanes, a young man who had been brought up in Prince Henry's household, did manage, after one unsuccessful attempt, to round that cape. What he did was to sail out to sea before he reached the cape and back to shore after he had passed it. This way he avoided the fierce northeast winds and dangerous currents beside the shore. And the big news was that the waters did not boil. His ship did not catch fire. The sea was navigable.

Gil Eanes had conquered what was perhaps the hardest part of the long African coastline. He had put to rest the old stories and taken some of the fear out of the Unknown. The next year Gil went back and sailed 150 miles farther than he'd been before. Gradually, Prince Henry's ships inched down the coastline.

Back in Portugal people were not interested in that coastline; they were complaining about how much money Prince Henry was spending. And for what? They could see no point in it. This didn't stop Prince Henry. In the first place, he wanted to find a route to those silks and spices. In addition, he wanted to take Christianity to the natives of Africa. Prince Henry was such a thoroughgoing Christian that he wore a prickly hair shirt next to his skin to remind himself that a Christian shouldn't be proud or too comfortable. But most important, Prince Henry wanted to solve the mystery of Africa. Now that Cape Bojador had been rounded, he told his men to find out what Africa was *like*. Bring back samples of everything they could find, he said. If they could bring back some African natives, he would be especially pleased. But he warned them not to use force. Just talk to them nicely.

In 1441 Antam Gonçalves, John's brother, delivered to Prince Henry some gold dust, a shield of oxhide, ostrich eggs, and ten Africans. Prince Henry was the first Christian prince to eat an ostrich egg and he declared that it was delicious. The people of Portugal, however, were more interested in those Africans. There was a severe labor shortage in

Portugal, and if Africans could be imported as slaves, the money Prince Henry was spending might not be wasted after all.

Before long, licenses were granted to Henry to send ships to Africa specifically to bring back slaves. On one of the first trips 165 men, women, and children were brought back. Another fleet returned with 235 natives. This was not done peacefully. Force was the only way to do it. But if Prince Henry regretted this, he probably comforted himself that he was "saving souls" by having the natives baptized. But the natives felt no comfort. As far as they were concerned, the arrival of the Europeans was bad news. And they would discover that the Europeans would go right on enslaving them. Europeans took for granted that other people were inferior because they were different, and so Europeans believed (or persuaded themselves) that they could use natives in whatever way that suited them. Once European curiosity was unleashed on the world, so was their cruelty, arrogance, and greed.

The African slave trade now became big business in Europe. This both encouraged and discouraged exploration. Some ships did venture farther, but some loaded up with slaves wherever they could get them and scurried home for a quick profit. Still, people were noticing that as they went down the African coast, it leaned more and more to the southeast. But how far did it go? Did it reach all the way to the South Pole? Did it swing around into the unknown land in the south and enclose the Indian Ocean? Ptolemy had thought so, but of course Europeans hoped for open sea between Africa and Asia.

Prince Henry never found out the answers. He died in 1460 at the age of sixty-six. He had brought 2,000 miles of the Unknown into the known world and in recent years had added the Cape Verde Islands and the Azores to the map.

After his death, Prince Henry became known as Prince Henry the Navigator, the man who set the Age of Exploration in motion.

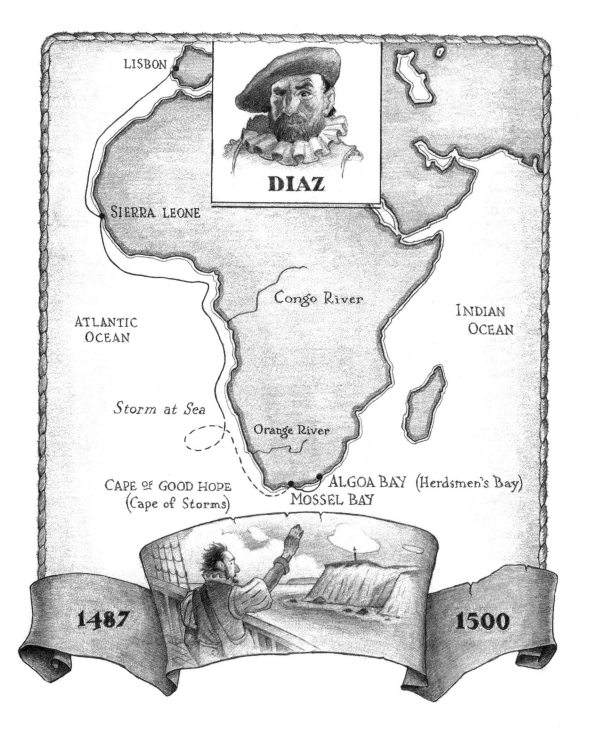

LISBON

DIAZ

SIERRA LEONE

Congo River

ATLANTIC
OCEAN

INDIAN
OCEAN

Storm at Sea

Orange River

CAPE OF GOOD HOPE
(Cape of Storms)

ALGOA BAY (Herdsmen's Bay)

MOSSEL BAY

1487

1500

3

Bartholomew Diaz

AFTER PRINCE HENRY'S DEATH, King Afonso took up the exploration and in five years lengthened the African coastline by another 1,500 miles. Still, the question of how far Africa extended south had not been answered. King John the Perfect, who came to the throne in 1481, was determined to find out. He wanted that spice trade, and since the land route to China had been closed by the Turks in 1453, the only way to go, King John figured, was by sea. He knew Africa must end somewhere, and if he could sail around it, perhaps he could cross the Indian Ocean to Calicut, a trading center that everyone knew was on the coast of India.

One thing, however, still hampered explorers. Normally, they fixed their position by looking at the North Star, but when they were south of the equator, the North Star disappeared. Only when they sailed close to the shore did they feel safe—in sight of land and the stone markers that previous explorers had set up as guideposts along the way. But sometimes they were driven into the open sea, and then what? Then all they could do was pray. How could they know where they were when the water was the same on all sides and the sky was like a foreign country that had betrayed them? So King John taught his explorers how to find their latitude by determining the height and angle of the midday sun and checking it against new charts that his astronomers had made.

Then he picked the man who was supposed to bring back the answers. The Diaz brothers were all explorers, but for this trip he chose Bartholomew Diaz, who had been in charge of the royal warehouses in Lisbon.

In August 1487 Bartholomew set sail with two caravels and a store ship carrying extra food and supplies. This was the first time a store ship had accompanied an expedition, so King John obviously expected Bartholomew to be away a long time. He also expected him to come home with answers. Spices and gold too.

No experienced sailor, however, could hope to be away long without running into a storm or two. Still, Bartholomew had never seen such a storm as swept his ships off the south-western coast of Africa. There they were, sailing peacefully along, their course set for the mouth of the Congo River, when all at once the world went mad. Mountains of water attacked them; the sky itself descended; the wind flung their ships about as if they were toys. And it became cold. They had been in the tropics when the storm hit, so how could it suddenly turn so cold? Where could they be? King John had told them to look at the midday sun. There was no midday sun. No night sky. They must be in the Unknown. It was easy enough to scoff at old stories about the

Unknown when they were on dry land, but not now. Not when they were on the brink of an icy death.

The storm raged for thirteen days, but when it was over, the two caravels were still afloat. The store ship was gone, but the men wouldn't need stores now. Surely their trip would be cut short. Surely they would go straight home. That is, if they could find home. Bartholomew Diaz studied the noonday sun and his charts and ordered the ships to go east. And they did. Day after day. But there was no land in the east. So Bartholomew said, Go north. Finally on February 3,

1488, they saw a bump of land sitting on the horizon, waiting for them like an old friend they had never expected to meet again. When they observed that the coastline continued north, they realized that they were on the other side of Africa. They had gone past the southern tip without even knowing it, and now they were going up the eastern shore. They were sailing in the Indian Ocean, and as far as they could tell, it was open sea.

Bartholomew dropped anchor and went ashore with his men to get fresh water and to put up a *padrão,* a stone marker, the first marker

on this side of Africa. He was proud of that marker, standing so tall on a green pasture among grazing cattle and naked herdsmen. He called the place Herdsmen's Bay, although the herdsmen had run off at the sight of strangers. Later, peeping over a hilltop, they threw stones down at the white men. Bartholomew did what Portuguese explorers had learned to do when Africans were not cooperative. He shot one of the herdsmen and the rest disappeared.

Bartholomew was ready now to sail up the coast and then across the Indian Ocean, but his men objected. Even the officers objected and threatened to mutiny. They'd had enough of the open sea; they knew the shape of Africa and that should satisfy King John. In the end, Bartholomew was forced to give in, but on one condition only. Each of his men would have to sign an oath, stating that Bartholomew Diaz was not responsible for changing the course. The men agreed, and reluctantly Bartholomew turned around. He hated to leave his stone marker behind. Looking at it, he said that he felt as though he were taking his "last leave of a son condemned to exile forever." To think, he said, that he'd come such a long way and "God would not grant it to me to reach my goal."

But at least on the way back they saw the point where Africa ended, which they had missed before. Africa did not just dribble away to nothing. Before it stopped going south and turned the corner to go north, it flung up a rocky cliff that jutted out to sea, a dramatic good-bye to the continent. Bartholomew called it the Cape of Storms, and landing nearby, he took sightings and drew a chart to show to King John.

Bartholomew Diaz and his two caravels arrived back in Portugal in December 1488. They had been away sixteen months and seventeen days and had added 1,400 new miles to the map. When Bartholomew made his report and showed his charts to the king, there was another

seaman who later claimed to be present, a man by the name of Christopher Columbus, well known in Portugal, who was now soliciting Queen Isabella of Spain to support a venture of his own. It was strange that King John would allow a potential competitor to look at those charts, since Portugal always tried to keep its discoveries secret. Yet Christopher Columbus claimed that he was present and did see just where Bartholomew Diaz had gone and what he had found.

Although King John was pleased with Bartholomew's charts, he did not care for the name that Bartholomew had given the cape at the tip of Africa. Who would seek a cape named the Cape of Storms? He renamed it the Cape of Good Hope.

Although Bartholomew Diaz was obviously the most experienced man to command the next expedition, he was not asked to do it. Instead he was given the job of supervising the building of ships. Perhaps the king thought Bartholomew had shown weakness when he turned back. In any case, King John became too busy with Portuguese troubles to go scouting for silks and spices. No one went to the Indies for another nine years.

Bartholomew Diaz, however, did have one more trip at sea. In 1500, when Pedro Cabral was given a fleet of thirteen ships to go to Calicut, Bartholomew had the command of one. He must have looked forward to greeting that stone marker he had planted, but he never had the chance. The fleet ran into a storm off the Cape of Good Hope. Four ships were lost and Bartholomew's was one of them. Although he had escaped death at sea once, he did not escape this time.

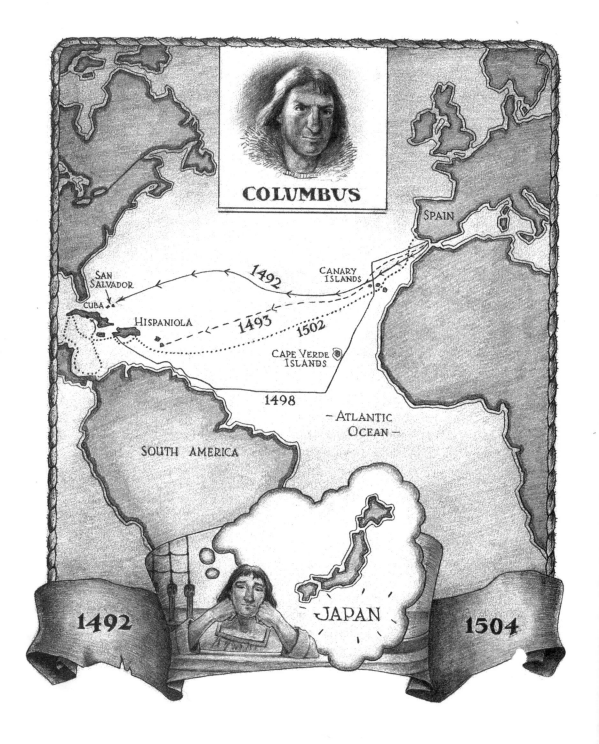

COLUMBUS

SPAIN

SAN
SALVADOR

CUBA

HISPANIOLA

1492

CANARY
ISLANDS

1493

1502

CAPE VERDE
ISLANDS

1498

– ATLANTIC
OCEAN –

SOUTH AMERICA

JAPAN

1492

1504

4

Christopher Columbus

CHRISTOPHER COLUMBUS WAS NOT SURPRISED that Bartholomew Diaz had found the way around Africa, but, Columbus insisted, that was the long way to the Indies. He wanted to go the short, easy way—past the Canary Islands, straight across the Ocean Sea, and on to the Indies. But so far no one was willing to send him. Ever since 1484 he'd been trying—first to persuade King John of Portugal to send him, then to persuade King Ferdinand and Queen Isabella of Spain. They said what everyone else said. The ocean was too wide. The winds didn't blow the right way to bring a ship back.

Christopher Columbus, who had been in love with the ocean all his life, had different ideas. Born in 1451 in the Italian seaport of Genoa, he went to sea early—first on short trips, then as far north as Iceland

and south down the west coast of Africa, learning how to handle a ship, how to deal with the ocean. And always longing to push back the horizon. In 1476 along with his brother Bartholomew, he set up a store in Lisbon, Portugal, to sell maps. Here he was surrounded by outlines of coasts, visions of the Known and the Unknown, by men who had skirted the horizon and had tales to tell.

In 1479 Christopher Columbus married Dona Felipa, the twenty-five-year-old daughter of Bartholomew Perestrelo, that shortsighted explorer who had taken a pregnant rabbit on his travels. Bartholomew had died when Felipa was about two years old, but Felipa's mother was living. And she told Columbus stories not only about Bartholomew but about her own father, who had been with Prince Henry when he had conquered Ceuta. Christopher and Felipa spent a few years in her mother's house on the island of Porto Santo, where their son Diego was born. Then they moved to Madeira. Christopher must have enjoyed living on an island with the horizon a wide circle of sea and sky around him. What he wanted to do, however, was to pull up anchor and sail beyond that circle.

Meanwhile he read. Perhaps his favorite book was the one that Marco Polo had written two hundred years before about his travels to China by the old land route. What Columbus liked best in Marco's book was his description of Japan (or Cipangu, as he called it). Marco hadn't actually been to Japan, but the way he told it, Japan sounded like a country practically paved with gold. Indeed, there was so much gold, he said, that whole palaces were built of it. This was exactly the kind of place that Columbus wanted to go to. Luckily it wasn't far. On Ptolemy's map the Ocean Sea didn't look hard to cross. Aristotle had figured that it would take only a few days. But the most impressive authority was Dr. Paolo Toscanelli, a famous Italian scientist. About 1481 Columbus wrote him a letter, and in reply Dr. Toscanelli stated that it was only about 3,000 nautical miles from the Canary Islands to Japan, going by way of the Antilles, one of those mythical island groups that no one had found but mapmakers said were there. And since the inhabitants of the Antilles were supposed to speak Portuguese, Columbus figured this would make a good rest stop.

No matter what anyone said, Columbus *knew* he was right. It was as if God had given him the true map of the world and told him where to go. Indeed, he boasted so much of his plans that people began calling him a show-off and a know-it-all. Queen Isabella, however, was too busy fighting a war to pay much attention to Columbus. She told him to wait and he waited six years. Not until Queen Isabella had finished her war did she finally say yes. She knew that if Columbus didn't come back, she would lose the ships she was giving him. But if he did come back! Think of the gold he'd have! She reminded Columbus to bring plenty of it. He promised he would. After all, he was going to a place where gold was as common as stones in Spain. He would bring back so much gold that Queen Isabella could make a final crusade and return Jerusalem to Christians, once and for all.

At eight o'clock on the morning of August 3, 1492, Christopher Columbus with his three ships—the *Niña,* the *Pinta,* and the *Santa María*—set sail, but it was not until September 6, when he left the Canary Islands, that he felt he was really on his way. Once in the open sea, Christopher Columbus took on new life as all born seamen do when they take the helm. Here he was in command of his destiny, in charge of the ocean, in league with the North Star, in service to the queen, under the orders of God Himself—the first man to cross the Ocean Sea. But if he was exhilarated by the expanse of water around him, his sailors weren't. They were used to being within striking distance of land; here they were not in striking distance of anything. Not even a rock poked through the water as a reminder of a stable world. Day and night the ship's boy called out the time as the sand trickled through the half-hour glass, but the half hours piled up and still only open sea lay around them. Where were the Antilles? The ships had long since passed where the Antilles were supposed to be; perhaps they had passed Japan too—if there was a Japan.

As the men became more and more fretful, Columbus worried. He certainly didn't want the same kind of trouble with his crew that had sent Bartholomew Diaz home early, so he took care to encourage his men. Not much longer, he would say. Already he had dropped 600 miles from Dr. Toscanelli's estimate, so according to his figures, they had only 2,400 miles to go. He pointed out favorable signs: land birds, a live crab, a floating stick that had been carved, perhaps, by Japanese. When the men became too restless, Christopher Columbus was firm. "*Adelante!* Sail on!" he would cry.

If Columbus could have shown his men the new globe made by the German cartographer Martin Behaim, this might have helped. Although the globe, which Behaim called an Earth Apple, had just appeared in 1492, Columbus undoubtedly knew about it and may even have seen it. There on that famous Earth Apple were the countries of the world arranged just as Columbus himself would have arranged them: a small ocean and Japan on a straight line west from the Canary Islands.

Finally, on the night on October 11, thirty-seven days after leaving the Canaries, an island broke through the horizon with a big, lopsided moon shining down on it. Columbus ordered his ships to drop anchor and wait for the morning, but surely he, along with many of his crew, stayed on deck all night, glorying in the sight before them. No one could doubt Columbus now. Of course this might not be Japan, and when he saw the naked people on the island, he realized that it wasn't. He knew the Japanese wore fancy clothes. But this island was close.

One of the many islands around Japan that Marco Polo had mentioned. Planting a flag, Columbus took possession of the island in the name of Spain and called it San Salvador. As part of the ceremony, he asked the Tainos, the people on the island, if they had any objections, but, as he reported later, they did not care. No one said a word. Of course if they had understood and objected, it would have made no difference to Columbus. It never occurred to him that a civilized, European nation didn't have the right to take over primitive lands, change their names, and rule their people.

Columbus never tired of planting his flags on the many islands that he found nearby. The islands seemed very much alike. The people were invariably friendly; the tropical trees were spectacular. But there was no gold. And although he knew he was sailing through the Indies, liable to bump into China or Japan at any moment, he *had* to find gold. When he came to the place that the local people called Colba (Cuba), he could see this wasn't Japan either, but it was big—bigger than any island in Europe—so he decided that it must not be an island at all. It must be part of the mainland of China, and if you went inland, you'd come to a place where people were dressed and lived a civilized life just as Marco Polo had described them. If this was China (and he knew it was), Japan must be right next door, so he sailed to the next island. No gold palaces here either. But at least there were small chunks of gold that the Tainos gave him. Best of all, they told him about a gold mine at the north end of the island.

Columbus named this island Hispaniola (now divided into Haiti and the Dominican Republic), and on the night of December 24, 1492, he headed north for that gold mine. On the way the *Santa María*, Columbus's ship, hit a reef and was hopelessly stranded. Everyone on the ship made it safely to shore, but what was Columbus to do? Where would he put all the men who had been on the *Santa María*? In the end, Columbus claimed that God told him what to do. He would build a fort and leave thirty-nine men behind to dig gold while he sailed back to Spain for more ships.

On his return to Spain in March 1493, Christopher Columbus received a hero's welcome and was addressed as "Admiral," "Viceroy," "Governor General"—the titles he had demanded and earned. All through Europe the news spread: The Ocean Sea had been crossed! Gold was waiting! Not everyone believed the stories, but King John of Portugal and Queen Isabella both wanted to make sure who could claim all the islands that were turning up. They asked the pope, Alexander VI, to settle the question. In 1494 Spain and Portugal signed a

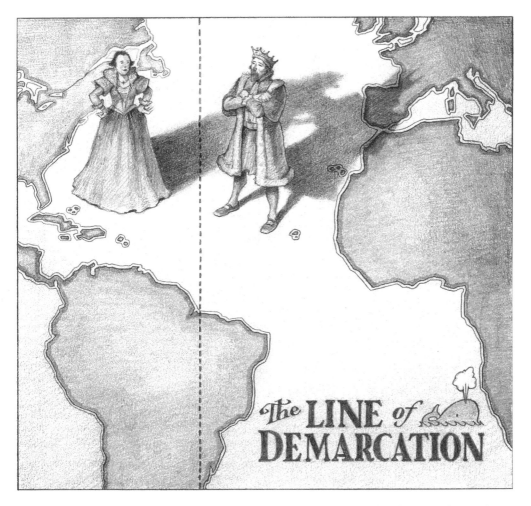

The LINE of DEMARCATION

treaty, agreeing on a line of demarcation that would be drawn through the New World. All lands 1,175 miles west of the Cape Verde Islands would belong to Spain. All lands east of this line would belong to Portugal. This was fine with Columbus. All those flags he had planted had a right to be there. And of course this sealed the fate of the original inhabitants. In the Christian world of the Europeans, the pope could decide what happened to people he had never seen and didn't know.

On September 25, 1493, Columbus and a fleet of seventeen ships left for his second trip while trumpets blared, lutes played, crowds shouted, and cannon boomed. On board were fifteen hundred men sent by the queen to build and colonize a town, to explore, and to dig for gold. Five men were assigned to the admiral as personal servants; six priests were included in addition to fifty horses and a pack of dogs trained to attack hostile natives if necessary. On the way Columbus planted forty-four flags on islands new to him. Everything was going well, just as he had expected.

On the night of November 27 the fleet anchored off the coast of Hispaniola at the site of the fort they had left, but when they sent up flares to announce their arrival, no answering flares greeted them. When they fired cannon, there was not a sound in reply. The next morning when they went ashore, there was nothing but scorched earth where the fort had been. A local chief, formerly friendly to Columbus, explained that the Spaniards had ransacked their villages, stolen their wives, demolished everything in their way. So the Spaniards had been killed. Every one of them.

That was the beginning of Columbus's troubles. Farther along the coast he built a settlement, which he called Isabela, but it was easy to see that Columbus could manage men at sea much better than he could on land. No one wanted to work or plant crops; they didn't even want to dig for gold. All they wanted was to collect it. When Columbus sent an expedition to locate the gold mine he'd been told about on his first trip, the men returned with the news that there was no gold mine. There was a little gold here and there in rocks and riverbeds, but they had not found enough even to fill a canoe. Yet Columbus had been told to load twelve ships with gold and send them back to Spain. He would have to send at least one ship back for supplies for his helpless settlers, but how could he send it back empty? So in addition to gold samples, he sent plants that looked as if they might be spices. And twenty-six Tainos. Later he would send a shipload of five hundred Tainos, and in

a desperate effort to find gold, he forced all Taino men over fourteen years old to fill small bells with gold and turn them over to the Spaniards. One bell per person every three months. This might not sound like much, but it was more gold than the island had. And if any man failed to deliver, he would be put to death.

Up until this time Columbus had made friends with the local people, and on many occasions he still did. On his landing at San Salvador he had reported that they were such a willing people, they would make good servants. But it was not as servants that Columbus was using them; it was as slaves. The Portuguese had done the same to the people they'd found in the Canary Islands and Africa, but Columbus, driven to distraction by the need for gold, introduced a brutal kind of slavery to this part of the world. Future explorers followed his example, often inflicting unspeakable cruelties, pointing out that what happened to heathens didn't matter. Indeed, these explorers had witnessed just such inhumanity in their own country against infidels of all kinds. Even now the Church was conducting a worldwide campaign called the Inquisition in order to track down and get rid of nonbelievers and heretics. Those who were found guilty were imprisoned, tortured, or killed. The most common method was to burn them at the stake. The explorers displayed the same kind of hard-heartedness. By 1500 the population of 25,000 native Tainos on Hispaniola had been reduced to a mere 5,000, and by 1520 the Tainos were virtually gone.

On this second trip to his islands, Columbus had been told to return to Colba or to what he called the mainland of China and make sure that it really was the mainland. Columbus was already sure, but obeying his instructions, he did follow the coastline—not all the way but farther than he'd been before. If he had gone 15 miles farther, he would have seen that although Colba was big, it was still an island. But he didn't want anyone to go back to Spain and contradict him, so he ordered all the men on this expedition to sign an oath, swearing that Colba was China. Anyone who broke his oath would be fined and have his tongue cut out.

By this time some settlers were so unhappy with Columbus that they stole a ship and sailed back to Spain to complain about what a bad governor he was. (And indeed he was.) In May 1496 Columbus returned to Spain to answer the charges. He must have been afraid that the queen would ground him, but instead she only warned him and in 1498 sent him back again. But the queen didn't trust Columbus as governor and appointed a new one, who was so eager to get rid of Columbus, he sent him home in chains. Again the queen overlooked his troubles and sent him on another trip in 1502. On this final trip, he reached the coast of what we now know as South America, but Columbus was confused by it. The only continent around was China, which was far to the north. It never occurred to Columbus that there could be a brand-new continent of which he'd never heard. This must be the Garden of Eden, he decided, which was supposed to be in the eastern part of the world. And this was east, as far east as Columbus could imagine. In any case, whatever the land was, it stood between Columbus and Japan, and he tried to find a way through it. Up and down the coast he sailed, searching for a strait. He never found one. And although he had crisscrossed his Indies again and again, he never found a gold palace either.

When he sailed back to Spain in 1504, he was fifty-four years old and in poor health. Still, he hoped to go out again, but Queen Isabella died before Columbus could reach her, and no one else seemed interested. Although by this time others had accepted the fact that there was indeed a new continent, Columbus never budged from his fixed ideas of geography. He had been to China, he insisted, and if he'd had more time, he would have reached Japan. In the last two years before he died in 1506, he felt sorry for himself. He talked as if he were not only unappreciated but poor. Of course he was not as rich as he thought he should be, but he was far from poor.

But if Columbus did not do all that he'd thought he'd done or wanted to do, what did he accomplish? He gave mapmakers a multitude of new islands. He enlarged the world by wiping the word "Unknown" off the Atlantic Ocean, and whether he would admit it or not, he led the way to the New World. As a result, the whole world was changed forever. Europeans considered this New World their own to explore, to exploit, to settle, to do with as they pleased. And the native peoples of this New World gradually lost their land, their peace, their freedom, and all too often their lives.

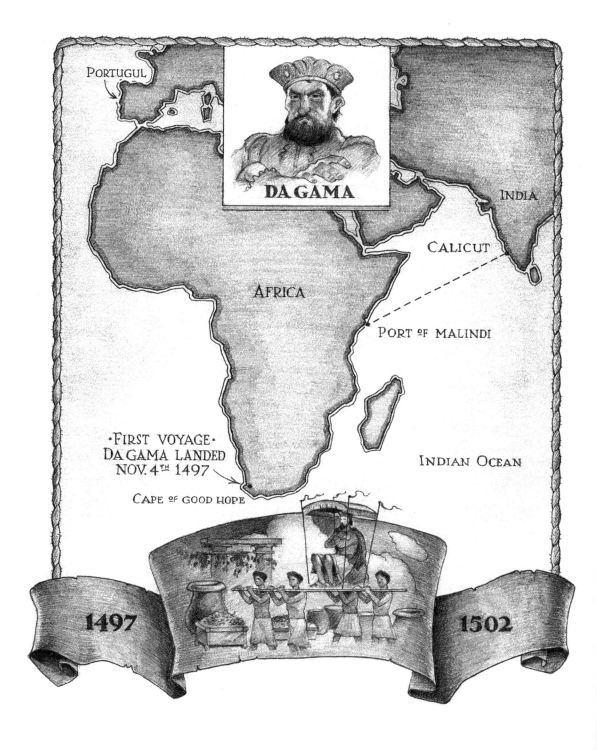

PORTUGUL

DA GAMA

INDIA

AFRICA

CALICUT

PORT ᴏꜰ MALINDI

·FIRST VOYAGE·
DA GAMA LANDED
NOV. 4ᵀᴴ 1497

CAPE ᴏꜰ GOOD HOPE

INDIAN OCEAN

1497

1502

5

Vasco da Gama

IN PORTUGAL King Manuel the Fortunate (who followed King John to the throne) had heard quite enough about Spain's new hero, Christopher Columbus, who had found a string of islands in the ocean. Not much treasure yet, but he promised to bring back more the next time—that is, if he could find it. But the Portuguese already knew exactly where treasure was and knew how to get there.

By 1497 King Manuel had an expedition fitted out, ready to follow Bartholomew Diaz's route around the Cape of Good Hope and then across the Indian Ocean to Calicut, that center for treasures on the southwest coast of India. Four ships were prepared for a three-year journey, and about 170 men signed up for it. Each ship was equipped with six anchors in case of loss and with twenty guns and many crossbows, javelins, pikes, and spears in case of trouble. And there was likely to be trouble. Calicut was ruled by Hindus, but its trade was largely controlled by Arabs—Muslims who didn't like Christian interference. Obviously, the leader of Manuel's expedition must be not only a fine seaman but also a soldier and a diplomat. Furthermore, he must be determined. No turning back on this trip. King Manuel chose Vasco da Gama, a thickset, hard-jawed man, born in 1460, the same year Prince Henry had died.

As it turned out, Christopher Columbus was in Spain in 1497, home from his second trip, so of course he knew about Vasco da Gama's expedition and looked forward to meeting him—not in Europe, but in the Indies. When Columbus returned to his islands in 1498, he carried a letter of introduction to Vasco da Gama to be delivered at sea. Although da Gama was going the long way and Christopher was going the short way, he figured that they were bound to bump into each other somewhere.

According to Vasco da Gama, he was going the *sure* way, and on June 8, 1497, he started out with just as grand a send-off as Columbus had been given on his second trip. Spectators crowded on the shore to watch the procession make its way to the waiting boats. First came the priests, chanting; then Vasco da Gama followed by his crew, two by two, all carrying lighted candles. When the four ships in the harbor actually sailed, trumpets blew and the people cheered. There go the Portuguese! On their way to show the world what treasure is!

Vasco da Gama proved to be a brave seaman and a good navigator. After his fleet made a short stopover at Cape Verde Islands, he decided to avoid the coastal storms that had plagued Bartholomew Diaz. He made a great loop west and south into the open sea, taking advantage of the circular trade winds that blew here. He returned to land on November 4 just north of the Cape of Good Hope. This was a longer

route, but it became the regular course that Portuguese ships would follow to the Indies. But the Cape of Good Hope, in spite of its name, was still a cape of storms, and Vasco da Gama had to wait until November 22 before the wind allowed him to round it and head north.

Three days later he was at Diaz's Herdsmen's Bay, where perhaps the happiest scene of his entire journey took place. Vasco da Gama was a stern, forbidding man, but apparently he was in a holiday mood and when two hundred friendly Africans staged a dance, he and his crew joined the circle and danced with them. Back on shipboard, he ordered his musicians to play Portuguese tunes and they continued to dance. Perhaps Vasco da Gama outstayed his welcome; in any case, he must have irritated the local people. As he was sailing away, he watched angry Africans tearing down the stone marker he had put up to replace the one that Bartholomew Diaz had left but that was no longer there.

Sailing far up the eastern coast of Africa, Vasco da Gama was in territory of which much was known to the Arabs but was new to those countries that faced the Atlantic Ocean, as well as to their mapmakers. Here da Gama saw things he had never seen before—melons, cucumbers, and coconuts, or "goblin" nuts, named because of their three eyes. Yet the sailors were uneasy. They were too far south to keep in touch with their familiar stars, although if anyone had felt like turning back, he never mentioned it. Vasco da Gama was not a man to be crossed.

The main concern now was finding a pilot to guide them across the sea to Calicut. Vasco da Gama didn't want to struggle through treacherous waters if an experienced navigator could steer them, but whenever he asked a local chief for a guide, he was given a runaround. Still, Vasco da Gama had his ways. And they were cruel. Whenever a native was uncooperative in giving help, da Gama ordered "the drops"—a mixture of boiling water and resin to be ladled onto his bare skin. Drop by drop. But not even "the drops" produced a pilot.

At last at the port of Malindi on the coast of what is now Kenya, there were many Indian ships at anchor, and Vasco da Gama could wait no longer. He captured a servant of the local sheik and held him hostage. Then at last a pilot was found. Da Gama may never have known that the pilot was a great Arab navigator who called himself the Lion of the Sea in Fury, and certainly the pilot didn't know that the man he was taking to Calicut would eventually destroy Arab trade in the Indian Ocean.

On April 24, 1498, Vasco da Gama and his four ships, led by the Lion of the Sea in Fury, set out for Calicut. It was an uneventful crossing except that soon after they had left Malindi, they recrossed the equator. And there were Orion, the Great Bear, and the North Star, back in place. It was almost as good as seeing Portugal. Since more and more

sailors had fallen sick with scurvy, a common disease at sea caused by lack of fresh fruit and vegetables (vitamin C), they were eager to go home. But first they wanted a chance at that treasure in Calicut. They had all brought with them private possessions of one sort or another to trade for spices and jewels. On May 20, 1498, Vasco da Gama dropped anchor at Calicut, and eight days later he was being carried in a fancy sedan chair (palanquin) to see the local Hindu king. Da Gama had every reason to think all was going well. On the one-day journey to the king's palace, crowds lined the road, beating drums, showing every sign of welcome, and indeed the king himself received

Vasco da Gama warmly. This, however, was only his first day at the palace.

The second day the king's Muslim officers told the Portuguese that now it was time for them to give the king presents. So Vasco da Gama displayed the gifts he had brought: twelve pieces of striped cloth, four scarlet hoods, six hats, four strings of coral, six basins, a case of sugar, two casks of oil, two casks of honey.

That was all? The king's officers were outraged. Such gifts were fit only for a native chief; for a civilized ruler, they were an insult. Where was the gold?

Vasco da Gama tried diplomacy. The Portuguese had not come to trade, he explained, only to explore. His excuse didn't work. The king was told that Vasco da Gama was nothing but a pirate, and from now on he was treated as such. When he returned to the shore, those crowds who had been so friendly taunted him. "Portugal! Portugal!" they cried, and spat on the ground. His sailors had managed to acquire small amounts of cloves and cinnamon and a few precious stones, and although Vasco da Gama had also gathered some treasure, it was not what he had expected. Yet when he was ready to leave, he was told he had to pay a tax on everything that he was taking. Instead, Vasco da Gama captured some hostages, and on August 23 he simply left. There was only one way to do business with Calicut, he decided. Conquer it. He'd come back with more ships and do just that.

His journey home was a hard one in which he lost so many men to scurvy that there were not enough left to sail four ships. He put everyone on two ships, burned the other two, and in August 1499 he finally arrived in Portugal with 55 survivors from the 170 men who had sailed with him.

In India he had left a trail of fear behind, but what had he accomplished? By proving once and for all that India could be reached by rounding Africa, he had finally made it possible for Europeans to buy spices without resorting to the high prices that Venice and Genoa charged. In addition, by making the longest voyage of any European vessel, he had shown that the ocean, though dangerous, could be challenged successfully.

Vasco da Gama himself was weakened by the trip and could not return to Calicut as soon as he might have liked. He did go back, however, in 1502 with twenty ships, determined to get even with those Muslims. This time he didn't wait for provocation. Not far from Calicut he stopped a large passenger ship on its way back from a pilgrimage to the Muslims' Holy City of Mecca. He took its cargo (money as well as valuables) and set the ship on fire, with 380 passengers locked up in the hold. When the passengers broke out and came on deck—women and children crying for mercy—Vasco da Gama showed no pity. For four days he stayed with the burning ship, firing at it again and again. Later, as he approached the city, he seized thirty-eight fishermen and hanged them from the rigging of his ship. The message he sent to the king was: Get rid of the Muslims. Then he sailed south to the neighboring state of Cochin, where he established friendly relations (and with other towns on the way), filled his ships with treasure, and sailed home.

Vasco da Gama gave up adventuring, but others continued, bringing much of India under Portugal's control to be ruled by a viceroy appointed by the Portuguese king. In 1524 the king decided that India was being mismanaged, so he asked Vasco da Gama to be the new viceroy. Vasco da Gama was sixty-four years old now, living in retirement with his wife and six sons, but if India needed to be set in order, he figured that he was the man to do it. He didn't have a chance to do much. On Christmas Eve, 1524, three months after his arrival, Vasco da Gama died after a short illness.

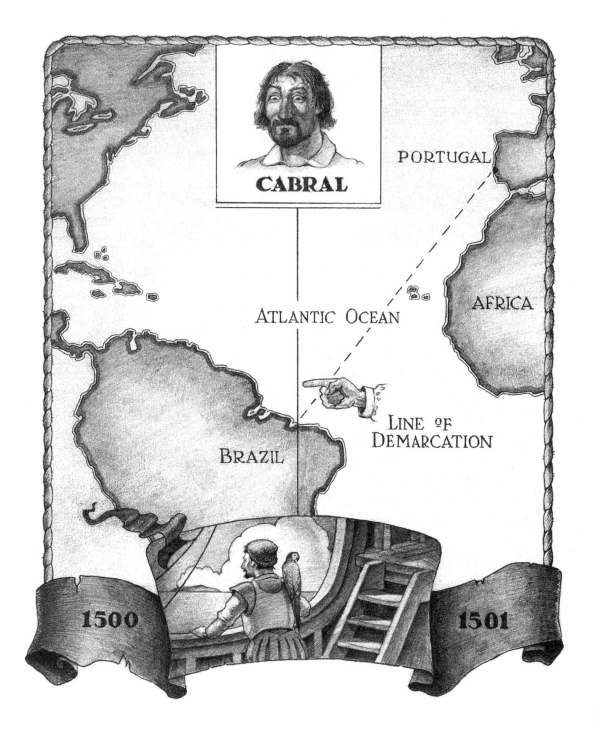

CABRAL

PORTUGAL

ATLANTIC OCEAN

AFRICA

LINE OF
DEMARCATION

BRAZIL

1500

1501

6

Pedro Álvares Cabral

AFTER VASCO DA GAMA HAD RETURNED from his first trip to Calicut, King Manuel, eager for a quick follow-up expedition, picked a thirty-two-year-old nobleman named Pedro Álvares Cabral for the job. He gave Cabral thirteen ships, at least three of which would be commanded by experienced explorers—Nicholas Coelho, who had sailed with Vasco da Gama, and two of the Diaz brothers, Diego and Bartholomew. The fleet sailed March 8, 1500, but not before da Gama made sure that Cabral knew how to make that loop into the ocean to pick up favorable winds off the African coast.

It was while he was on this loop that Cabral made history—quite by accident, which, of course, is the way history is often made. The winds were not only favorable but strong, sending him farther and farther west beyond the point he had expected to loop back. Then suddenly in the midst of an empty ocean a tall cone-shaped mountain erupted into view. Cabral had not expected to see land here, but since it was definitely land and since this was Easter week, he named it Easter Mountain (Mount Pascoal). At first he thought this was an island, but it turned out to be a great bulge on the coastline that must be on the edge of a continent. In any case, whatever it was, Cabral decided to claim it for Portugal. And he had every right to do so, because he was on Portugal's side of the line that the pope had drawn. Up to this time all newly found lands in this area had fallen to Spain, but here he was putting Portugal on the map. He was so excited that he sent one of his ships back to King Manuel with the good news.

There was only one problem. Not expecting to come across new land, Cabral had brought with him no stone markers, so he made do with a giant wooden cross that was put together by his men. He planted it with the usual ceremony, and then and there Portugal became a part of what would soon be called the New World. Sometimes on early maps this land was called the Land of Parrots. (Cabral brought parrots home with him.) Sometimes it was simply noted that it was Portuguese land. For the first time on a map in 1511 it was called Brazil, named for its famous brazilwood, used to make a red dye.

Cabral took a short vacation in his new land, going ashore to be entertained by the local people. Diego Diaz danced with them and invited them aboard ship. (When they lay down on the deck after feasting, Cabral's men were so embarrassed by all that stretched-out nudity, they covered the people with blankets.) But after ten days, when Cabral set sail for India, the fun was over. There was nothing now but disaster—storms in which six ships were lost (including the one that Bartholomew Diaz was on) and a war with Calicut. Still, on his return to Portugal in 1501, five of his ships were loaded with spices

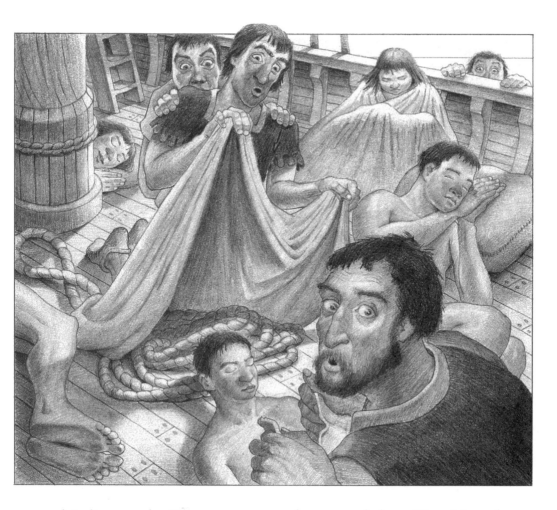

and Indian goods. Two were empty, but nevertheless, King Manuel was pleased. Not only had Cabral planted Portugal's cross in a distant land, he had proved that a regular trade around Africa to the Indies was possible.

King Manuel told Cabral to prepare for a return trip. For eight months he worked, but at the last minute Vasco da Gama, who was superior in rank, decided that he would take over this expedition. And he did. Cabral retired from the sea, married, had six children, and in 1530 he died at the age of sixty-three.

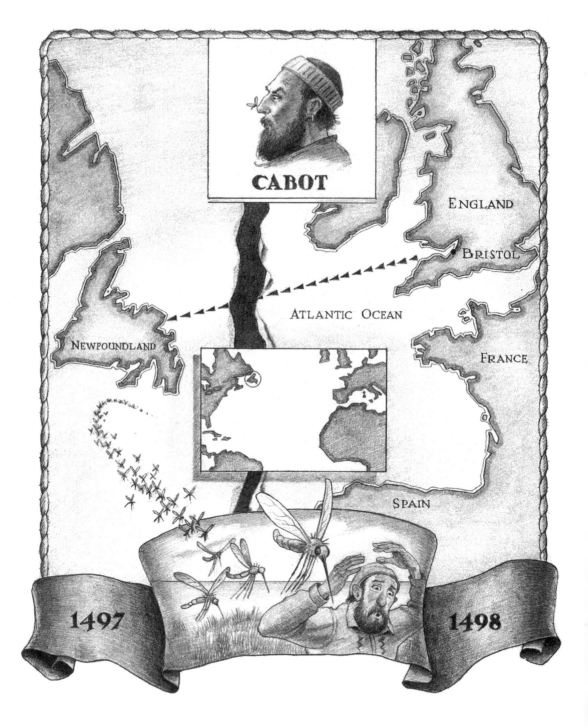

CABOT

ENGLAND

BRISTOL

ATLANTIC OCEAN

NEWFOUNDLAND

FRANCE

SPAIN

1497

1498

7

John Cabot

WHEN CHRISTOPHER COLUMBUS RETURNED from his first voyage and news spread of his successful crossing of the Ocean Sea, other explorers were eager to join the race to the Indies. John Cabot was one. Born in Genoa, Italy, about 1451, the year that Columbus was born, he may have known Columbus as a young boy, but if so, there is no record of it. In any case, when he was ten, he moved with his family to Venice, that great European trade center and seaport where it would be hard for a young man not to feel that he was on the edge of adventure.

John Cabot began his adventures early. Although we don't know about all his journeys, we do know that once he sailed down the Red Sea to the Muslims' Holy City of Mecca. At one time Mecca was the destination of overland caravans returning from China, but Europeans had been forced to abandon all overland travel after the fall of Constantinople, so Cabot was interested in finding what he could about where these spices and silks came from. For some reason he got the impression that they came from northern China. So when Columbus returned from his first voyage, John Cabot decided that Columbus was going the wrong way. It was no wonder that all he found was islands; he was too far south to find much else. John Cabot, however, planned to sail through northern waters on a shortcut that would take him straight to north China, where the treasure was.

Sometime between 1493 and 1495 John Cabot moved his wife and three sons to England and settled in the famous seaport of Bristol. He had decided that England would be the logical country to sponsor his trip. Since the English were at the far end of the trade route and had to settle with so many middlemen on the way, they had to pay more for their spices than anyone else. John Cabot wasted no time in going to London to see King Henry VII, who was indeed interested. King Henry was sorry that he had turned down Christopher Columbus's brother Bartholomew, who had once asked him to sponsor the Columbus trip. But now with the help of his "well beloved" John Cabot (as he called him), he might end up with an even quicker route to the Indies.

On March 5, 1496, the king promised John Cabot five ships "to seeke out, discover, and finde" territory previously unknown to Christians. But for some reason, when Cabot actually sailed from Bristol on May 20, 1497, he had only one small ship, the *Mathew,* and a crew of eighteen. Obviously he couldn't spend much time scouting around for jewels and spices, but if he at least found the way, if he touched on a Chinese shore, he could return with more ships to do serious business.

At five o'clock on the morning of June 24, land was sighted, and since it was St. John's Day, he named it St. John and went ashore to take possession. He meant the name to apply only to the place where he had landed, because he assumed the country was China. But as he sailed south down the coast, he could see that this was not the mainland. He, too, had found only an island, but it was a big one. It took him about a month to sail to the southern tip and back, and he saw just how on his next trip he could sail around it to the mainland.

He arrived back in Bristol on August 6, 1497, so full of glowing descriptions of what he had seen that King Henry VII was soon referring proudly to this territory as his "new founde land." Gradually this became "Newfoundland," and eventually it was a province in eastern Canada. Like all explorers, John Cabot wanted to present the best picture of his findings, so if he ran into the dense fog that hugs the Newfoundland coast (and he must have), he didn't mention it. If he was attacked by armies of mosquitoes, which still infest the land (and he must have), he said nothing. He didn't even refer to the icebergs which he surely saw and which probably kept him from going through the nearby Strait of Belle Isle, the shortest way around the island.

In a letter to Christopher Columbus (written in 1497–98), John Day, a trader who had obviously talked to Cabot or his shipmates, described what Cabot had seen: "big trees from which the masts of ships are made," "a spot where someone had made a fire," "dung of animals which they judge to be tame," "vegetation which appeared fair to them," and a "stick of elbow length perforated at both ends and painted with brasil [red]." In other words, Cabot judged the lands to be inhabited, and because he had so few men, they didn't dare proceed beyond a crossbow shot from the ship. John Day didn't mention that there was such an abundance of codfish that the men could catch all they wanted simply by lowering baskets into the water. On the whole, John Day made light of the expedition. "The people whom he engaged disconcerted him [made trouble for him]," he said, "and he went ill provisioned and encountered contrary winds and decided to return."

King Henry, however, did not make light of John Cabot's trip. He gave him ten pounds as a reward and an annual pension of twenty pounds, and he began right away to dream of a new colony that would make London the greatest center for spice trade in the world. On February 3, 1498, he gave Cabot the power to impress six English ships for a new venture.

John Cabot was equally pleased with himself. During the winter of 1497–98 he paraded about London in rich-looking silks, calling himself "Admiral" and promising to give away islands, even to his barber. Wherever he went, he was followed by ogling crowds. He didn't mind this one bit.

At the beginning of May 1498, John Cabot was ready for his return voyage. His six ships sailed out of Bristol harbor, and although one ship ran into trouble off Ireland and had to return, the rest went on. And not one of them was ever heard from again. Back in England people said that if John Cabot found land, it was at the bottom of the sea.

From his first trip to his "new founde land," John Cabot or a member of his crew left behind, probably by accident, a broken gilt sword and a pair of silver earrings, both made in Venice. They were picked up and taken to Lisbon by a group of Beothuk Indians captured by a Portuguese explorer who went to Newfoundland in 1501. Indeed, for a short period the Portuguese, cut off by the Spanish from explorations in the Caribbean, concentrated on northern voyages. In 1500 men from the Azores sighted what is the island of Greenland, but they called it Labrador because it was first seen by John Fernandes, who, as it happened, was a *lavrador,* or farmer. It was not until almost one hundred years later that Sir Martin Frobisher, an English explorer, discovered that Labrador had originally been called Greenland by the Norse who settled there. Mapmakers restored that name and moved Labrador over to the Canadian coast where it now is.

Lands in the North Atlantic were gradually taking shape, and fortunately John Cabot left behind a map of where he had been. A mapmaker, Juan de la Cosa, who was said to have sailed with Columbus on his second voyage, apparently saw the map and entered Cabot's findings on a world map which he drew and which appeared about 1505. This map definitely showed that Cuba was an island, even though Juan de la Cosa was one of those who had been sworn by Columbus to say that it was not. But what could Columbus do? It was too late to cut anyone's tongue out. And as for John Cabot's original map, no one knows what happened to it.

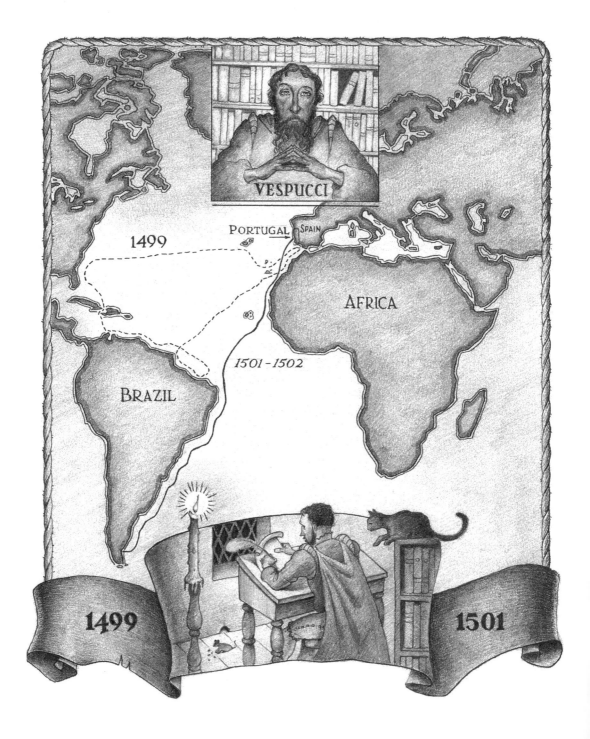

VESPUCCI

1499

PORTUGAL SPAIN

AFRICA

1501 - 1502

BRAZIL

1499   1501

8

Amerigo Vespucci

THE CITY OF ISABELA that Columbus built on Hispaniola became a center for traders, explorers, and for Spaniards who hoped to get rich quickly. The city looked respectable with its square plaza and church and a stone palace for the governor. (The governor was of course Columbus.) But right from the start, the colony had trouble. The colonists didn't like to work; they kept getting sick; they ran out of food; they couldn't get along with each other or with Columbus. When Columbus went exploring and left the colony in charge of his brother Diego, the colonists didn't get along with him either. Neither man was good at maintaining order, but worse than that, they were from Genoa. Spaniards saw no reason to obey foreigners, especially ones who promised so much and produced so little. Perhaps the settlers were by nature

difficult men. A historian writing in 1525 thought so. No early governor of Hispaniola, he said, could have succeeded unless he were super-
human.

Still, this was the place where explorers stopped, met, exchanged
news, loaded up with supplies, and repaired their ships. When the
capital was moved from Isabela to Santo Domingo, this became the
explorers' headquarters. One of the most interesting visitors and certainly the most controversial was Amerigo Vespucci. Historians still
argue about him. Some give him credit for recognizing a continent
when he saw one. Others call Amerigo Vespucci an out-and-out faker.

But there are some facts that no one disputes. Born in 1454, Amerigo
Vespucci came from a prominent family in Florence, Italy, and was a
friend of Lorenzo Piero de Medici, ruler of Florence. Always interested
in maps and astronomy, Vespucci followed news of explorations av-
idly, and when Columbus was preparing for his third voyage, Amerigo
Vespucci helped to outfit his ships. The next year, 1499, he himself
went exploring. According to some historians, Vespucci went as a
gentleman tourist on an expedition commanded by Alonso de Ojeda.
According to others, he was expected to make astronomical observa-
tions and was given directional charge of at least some of the ships. He
was particularly interested in locating a star that he imagined must
remain fixed at the South Pole as the North Star was fixed at the North
Pole. In any case, when Alonso de Ojeda and Amerigo Vespucci
reached the area that Columbus had called the Garden of Eden (somewhere on the coast of Suriname or French Guiana), Vespucci went
south down the coast and Ojeda went north in search of pearls. They
did eventually meet up in Hispaniola, and Vespucci sailed back to
Spain several months after Ojeda.

On his return, Amerigo Vespucci wrote a long letter to his friend
Lorenzo, describing his experiences on the mainland, which he called

"at the extreme limits of Asia." Unfortunately, he had been forced by strong currents to turn back before he could locate the star or group of southern stars that he was seeking. If he could only find that star, he thought, he could solve the problem of longitude and so immortalize his name. If his letter seemed long-winded, he suggested that his friend read it at the end of dinner when he was in a mood for "belching."

Meanwhile, Amerigo Vespucci was going over his figures to establish exactly where he'd been. To his surprise, he discovered that without knowing it, he had crossed the Line of Demarcation into Portugal's territory. Indeed, he had seen the north end of Brazil before any other European had seen it, ten months before Cabral. By this time King Manuel of Portugal had received word of Cabral's landing in Brazil and was eager to find out just how much property he owned across the sea. Vespucci wanted to return and was willing to sail under the Portuguese flag, so King Manuel gave him ships and asked him to check the Brazil stories. It was to be a trip "solely to make discoveries and not to seek any profit." This pleased Vespucci. Unlike other explorers, he was no gold seeker. He was curious, as well as being eager for fame. Perhaps he would achieve fame if he had another chance to study those southern stars. Or if he was able to find the strait that Columbus had failed to find.

Amerigo Vespucci had what sounds like one of the happiest explorations of his time. Right from the start he was lucky. When he reached the Cape Verde Islands, there was Pedro Cabral returning from India. Of course Vespucci was full of questions about Brazil. And of course Cabral was eager to hear the latest news from Portugal. Then off Vespucci sailed for Brazil, the land that had captured his imagination. Although he mapped the Portuguese territory, naming the harbors and rivers as he proceeded down the coast, he took time to marvel at the sights. Indeed, he spent twenty-seven days living among the native peoples, observing how they lived, ate, loved, played, made war with other tribes. He noted that they had no king, no laws, no religion, no private property, yet seemed to live at peace among themselves. As for other forms of natural life, he was lost in wonder. The multitude of brilliantly colored birds! The variety of animals! There were so many

species, he said, they could never have fitted on Noah's ark. In addition, he contended that there were far more languages in the world than anyone had imagined. Scholars generally agreed that there were seventy-seven languages, but Vespucci thought that there were at least one thousand.

Amerigo Vespucci traveled south for nine months and twenty-seven days, giving mapmakers about 3,300 new miles to add to their maps, but he did not find his fixed star. He thought he'd made some advance in determining longitude by recording the time it took the moon to pass certain planets, but no accurate measurement of longitude was established until 1735, when one John Harrison invented a chronometer, the first instrument that could measure time correctly on a rolling ship.

Nor did Vespucci find a strait. He went far below the Portuguese territory, sailing quickly, because this land belonged to Spain. Still there was no strait. But since the coast continued unbroken for so long, he came to the conclusion that this was a new continent, previously unknown. At least so he wrote to Lorenzo in 1502.

And now the controversy really begins. Lorenzo died in 1503. According to one theory, someone who was familiar with Vespucci's letters decided that they should be printed. Readers in Europe were hungry for news of the strange world across the sea. The stranger, the better. So the editors added juicy bits, exaggerated Vespucci's descriptions, and changed the geographical data so that it was not only false but contradictory. In some cases they even used careless language such as Vespucci never would have used. Was Amerigo Vespucci really a boaster? No one knows, but the editors had him boasting that he was "more skilled than all the shipmates of the whole world." The most dramatic thing they did, however (if they did it), was to change the date of his voyage to the new continent to 1497, one year before Columbus had actually been there. This of course made Amerigo Vespucci the

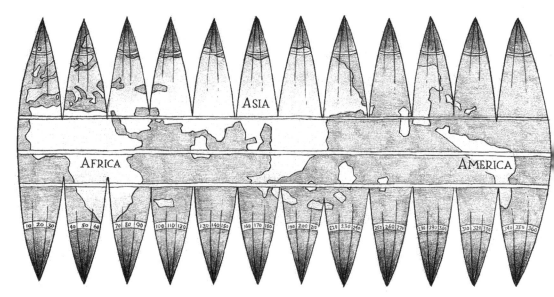

MARTIN WALDSEEMÜLLER'S MAP

"discoverer," and many people reading the two printed letters believed this.

Some historians insist that these published accounts, which came out in 1504, were actually written by Vespucci. Some claim they were forgeries. Martin Waldseemüller, a German mapmaker, believed in them. In 1507 he was making a world map in which he showed a continent between Europe and Asia. It was a very narrow continent blocking the way to Asia, and just beyond its borders in a hitherto unknown sea was an oblong island marked Cipangu, or Japan. Martin Waldseemüller loved making up names, so when he read these accounts written or supposedly written by Amerigo Vespucci, he was delighted. Now he could give that southern continent a name. Right across Brazil he splashed the word *America*. It was a good name for a continent, he thought, ending with an *a* just like Africa and Asia. And unlike Europe and Asia, it was named for a man. About time! he said.

On their maps Spaniards went on calling the continent either the New World or the Indies. And on a later version of his map, Waldseemüller, perhaps thinking he had not been fair to Columbus, removed the name *America*. But it was too late. The name had caught on, and before long it was applied to all the land in the Western Hemisphere.

As for Columbus, he died the year before Martin Waldseemüller's map came out, so there was no chance of it upsetting the friendship between him and Amerigo Vespucci, which continued through the last days of Columbus's life.

PONCE DE LEÓN

NORTH
ATLANTIC

FLORIDA

CUBA

PUERTO RICO

YUCATAN

SOUTH
ATLANTIC

PACIFIC
OCEAN

DISCOVERER
OF
FLORIDA

1513

9

Juan Ponce de León

EXPLORERS WERE RANGING ALL OVER THE SEA that Columbus had always called *his* sea, but what of the land north of that sea? John Cabot had explored far to the north, but what about the continent, if that's what it was, that lay in between? Settlers on the islands knew that there was some sort of land there. Not only had natives told them but navigators who had gone off on their own had sighted land. A map published in 1502 indicated a stray jut of land, pointing south. Whatever it was, it hadn't been officially claimed.

Juan Ponce de León had been living in Hispaniola since arriving with Columbus in 1493, and he was interested in that land. And not only the land. Somewhere on that land there was supposed to be a magic fountain that made old people young and kept young people young if they drank from it. People said it might be on an island called Bimini. Or on another nearby island.

But before Ponce de León could look for the fountain, the king of Spain sent him to conquer the island of Puerto Rico. Of course his famous red-coated dog, Bercerillo, went with him. Not only was Bercerillo said to be the equal of fifty men in a fight, he could tell with a single sniff if a stranger was friendly or unfriendly. As it turned out, most of the people on Puerto Rico (also Tainos) were unfriendly, but Ponce de León himself was not friendly either. In any case, he conquered the Tainos and for three years ruled the island. Still, off in the distance he kept hearing that gush of water, that splash of promise—the sound of old age washing away.

On March 3, 1513, with the permission of the king, Ponce de León set out at last to follow his dream. And none too soon. He was thirty-nine years old now, not really old but not really young either. With three ships he sailed north, picking his way among the islands scattered like grazing sheep across the sea. On April 3, after just a month at sea, he dropped anchor and went ashore on what seemed to be a large island. A beautiful island so ablaze with wildflowers and blossoming trees, it appeared to be the very home of springtime. The air smelled sweet. And young. Just the kind of place a person might expect to find a magic fountain. Ponce de León planted a cross and claimed the land for Spain. Because it was the Easter season (*Pascua florida,* or "flowering Easter"), he called it La Florida. But there was no sign of gushing water.

Down the coast he sailed, stopping at every village to ask about a fountain. Not only did the people not know about any fountain, they didn't like Spaniards bursting in on them. They didn't want Spaniards even to come near. Actually, Ponce de León need not even have asked. If there had been a magic fountain nearby, there would not have been old people in the village. And there were. Still, he kept asking. Only once did his hopes rise. Stopping at a tiny island known now as Key Biscayne, he came upon a clear, bubbling spring. It was not a fountain but it was so crystal-like, so dancing with sunlight, it looked as if it might have been a fountain once. Eagerly, Ponce de León and his men leaned down and scooped up handfuls of water. They slurped it down. Then they stood, looking at each other, waiting for something to happen. Nothing did.

On they sailed. Around the southern tip of Florida. Up the west side. Before going back to Puerto Rico, Ponce de León sent one of his ships to search for the island of Bimini while he went south and west. Still hoping. When he came to land, he mistook it for Cuba or an island off Cuba. Just in case, he named it Bimini, but when he and his men left, they were all just as old as when they had come. As it happened, this land was the Yucatán peninsula, and without knowing it, Ponce de León was the first European to step on what would later be called Mexico.

Back in Puerto Rico, Ponce de León kept thinking about Florida. Not about the Fountain of Youth. As the years went by, he gave up on that. Perhaps people teased him about his early dreams. That fountain, they would have said, was just a story. Too strange to be true. But what was too strange? Was it any stranger than a new world suddenly popping out of the Ocean Sea?

By the time Ponce de León was forty-seven years old, he had resigned himself to the idea of old age, but he did want to spend his last years in Florida. After all, he'd found the place, claimed it, and now he wanted to plant a colony on it. He also wanted to find out if Florida was an island or not. On February 21, 1521, he set out with two hundred men, fifty horses, cattle, sheep, and swine and landed on the beautiful shell-strewn beach that we now call Sanibel Island. But the native people of Florida were no happier to see Spaniards now than they had ever been. Hardly had the colonists started to put up their houses before angry natives descended upon them, bows drawn, arrows flying. One of the arrows buried itself deep in Ponce de León's flesh. It was a serious wound that not only wouldn't heal but became dangerously infected. The colonists decided that Florida was not for them. So they boarded their ships and sailed to the nearest settlement in Cuba. Ponce de León's wound never did heal and he died in Cuba, still not sure if Florida was an island or not.

Alonso Álvarez de Pineda was the one who settled the island question. He was one of many explorers looking for a strait that would lead quickly to China. There must be such a strait, explorers figured—some way through this inconvenient mass of land that was keeping them from where they wanted to go. On his search Pineda mapped the shore of the Gulf of Mexico and encountered a mighty river which would later be called the Mississippi. Pineda came upon no strait, but he did determine that Florida was part of the mainland. But how far north did Florida go? Even if he wanted to find out, Pineda couldn't have. He was killed, scalped, and skinned by native people in Texas, who, like those in Florida, wanted to keep their own land. Spanish mapmakers, however, decided that Florida, which was their territory, just kept on going up the eastern coast of North America. Indeed, even a century later when the English settled in Jamestown, Virginia, Spaniards accused them of trespassing on Spanish territory.

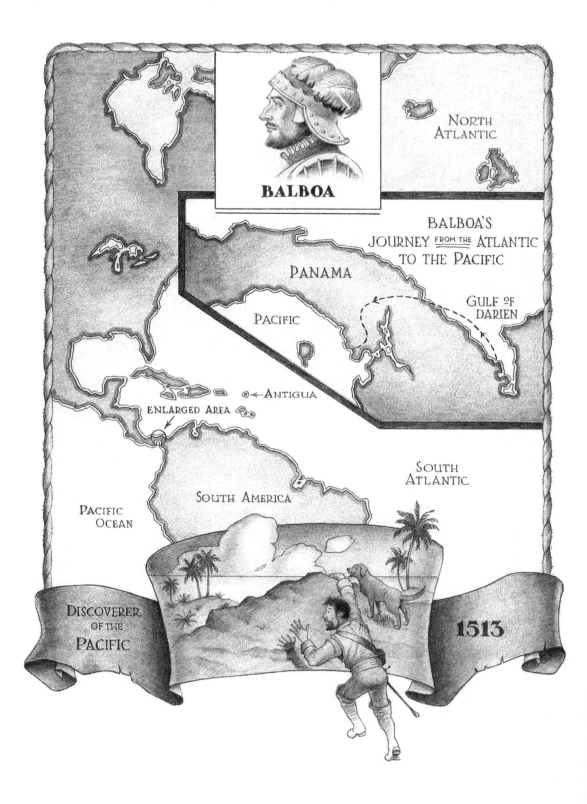

BALBOA

NORTH ATLANTIC

BALBOA'S JOURNEY FROM THE ATLANTIC TO THE PACIFIC

PANAMA

GULF OF DARIEN

PACIFIC

←ANTIGUA

ENLARGED AREA

SOUTH ATLANTIC

PACIFIC OCEAN

SOUTH AMERICA

DISCOVERER OF THE PACIFIC

1513

10

Vasco Núñez de Balboa

AFTER COLUMBUS HAD RETURNED from his third voyage and reported seeing pearls and gold in what he thought was the Garden of Eden, explorers rushed to the site. Indeed, how could an adventurous man resist? Among the first to go was a twenty-five-year-old fencing master, a blond, good-looking man named Vasco Núñez de Balboa. He left Spain in 1500 with an expedition headed by Rodrigo de Bastidas, who had seen Columbus's chart of 1498 and knew how to get to the Gulf of Darién, where the Isthmus of Panama joins the South American mainland. This is where the pearls and gold were. Bastidas loaded up, explored the coast of what is now Colombia, and headed home. On his way his two ships crashed into rocks at the extreme western tip of

Hispaniola. Bastidas and his men got to shore safely, but captive slaves on board, with their legs in chains, were left to go down with the ships. But not the pearls and the gold. The men managed to save them. They carried those heavy treasure chests all the way across the island to the new capital, Santo Domingo.

If he had to be shipwrecked, Balboa had found a convenient place. As unruly as the island was, a new system had recently been introduced in which each settler was given a plot of cultivated land, complete with ten thousand cassava plants and all the Tainos who lived on it. The owner could use those Tainos as he pleased. Since Balboa was not ready to leave the New World, he decided to become a settler. He moved in with his cassava plants and his slaves, making friends, running his farm, and hoping somehow to go exploring again. Balboa was a hard worker, yet for some reason he kept running into debt. And the rule was: No one who was in debt was allowed to leave the island. Balboa watched people come and go from Santo Domingo while he stayed and stayed. For seven years he stayed. Even his friend Ponce de León left to conquer Puerto Rico. Before leaving he gave Balboa one of Bercerillo's pups. Balboa named him Leoncico after his friend, and together they stayed, trapped with ten thousand cassava plants and those stubborn debts.

In 1509 Alonso de Ojeda suddenly turned up in Santo Domingo, looking for recruits for a new colony. Everyone knew Ojeda, at least by reputation. He had proved himself a fierce and cruel fighter on Columbus's second voyage, had been in Santo Domingo in 1499 with Amerigo Vespucci, and was there again in 1502 when his captains had mutinied and brought him in shackles to be jailed. And now here he was, back with an appointment as governor of a new colony to be established in the area around the Gulf of Darién near where Balboa had been.

Ojeda was to share the governorship with Diego de Nicuesa, another unsavory character, who was already at Santo Domingo, but when the two men met, they couldn't stand each other, so they decided to divide their territory between them. Ojeda would rule the eastern side of the gulf, and Nicuesa would rule the western side. They invited Martín de Enciso to join them as a third partner to follow later with more recruits and supplies.

If it hadn't been for his debts, Balboa would have jumped at the chance to sign up as a recruit, no matter how unpleasant the leaders were. Anything would be better than rotting here forever with his cassava plants, but the only way he could leave the island would be to sneak away. He'd have to become a stowaway. He enlisted the help of a friend who agreed to smuggle his two most precious possessions on board Enciso's ship—his sword and Leoncico. And Balboa hid himself in a barrel. When the other barrels filled with supplies were rolled on

deck, so was the barrel filled with Balboa. He stayed scrunched up in his hiding place until he felt the ship sail and was sure that Enciso had gone too far to be willing to turn back. Then he let himself out.

Enciso was furious. If there was one thing he didn't want, it was a man who would argue with him. Yet that is exactly what he got. Balboa told Enciso to settle on the west side of the gulf because on his previous trip he'd heard that the people there did not use poisoned arrows. Those on the east side did. Enciso didn't like the idea of poisoned arrows, so he took the suggestion. They named their settlement Santa María de l'Antigua del Darién, or simply Antigua for short.

Then there was the question of government. Enciso said he was in charge and all the gold and pearls found would belong to him. Balboa argued. Since neither Ojeda nor Nicuesa was there, he said, the place belonged to no one. The settlers should elect their leader. And they did. They elected Balboa.

Not surprisingly, the three original leaders of the expedition not only caused trouble, they got into it. Enciso made so much trouble that Balboa's men expelled him and he headed back to Spain. And Ojeda, the famous Indian fighter, had to run for his life from men on the east side who had poisoned arrows. As for Nicuesa, he was doing so poorly in his settlement down the coast that he moved to Balboa's colony, but the colonists didn't want him. They told him to get out, and when he didn't, they chased him down the beach, forced him into a leaky boat, and pushed him out to sea. He was never heard from again.

On December 23, 1511, King Ferdinand of Spain appointed Balboa acting governor of Darién. Compared to other Spanish governors, Balboa was a good one and well liked. Most Spaniards took for granted that natives should be fought and turned into slaves. What else were they good for? Although Balboa was not afraid to fight if necessary, he preferred to make friends with local people and avoid violence

if possible. He was a firm man but a kind one, and within a short time he was on such good terms with Careta, a nearby chief, that he became his blood brother. When he married the chief's beautiful daughter, Caretita, he treated her as a true wife. For her part, she was loyal and counseled him well on how to deal with her people. Both father and daughter were given Christian baptism, and while Careta agreed to supply the Spaniards with food, Balboa agreed to help Careta fight his enemies.

It was, however, when Balboa was visiting the palace of a distant chief, Comagre, that his career as an explorer took its most promising turn. Comagre and his seven sons were so friendly that they distributed gold to Balboa's men, but at the sight of gold the Spaniards became as quarrelsome and greedy as spoiled children. Who had the most gold? Were the shares equally divided? Could they have more? Comagre's oldest son was disgusted. "If you love gold so much," he said, "I'll show you more." He offered to take them to another sea. The people there were very rich and had gold mines, he said.

Another sea! A gold mine! Balboa was so excited that he ordered Comagre and all his sons to be baptized immediately. He gave Comagre the Christian name of Carlos. It would be a difficult trip, Carlos explained—across mountains, through swamps, in forests too thick to let in sunshine. And since there were cannibals on the way, Balboa would need to take a thousand soldiers with him. Balboa rushed back to Antigua and wrote to the king of Spain, telling him the good news and asking for one thousand men to make the trip across that narrow neck of land that we now call Panama. As the people waited for the king's reply, all they talked about was the gold, the pearls, the spices that awaited them.

The king was delighted with Balboa's news, but by this time Enciso had arrived in Spain and charged Balboa with crimes he had never committed. The king believed him. Obviously, the king was not pleased, and rumors of his displeasure reached Balboa. There was even talk that the king would send another governor to take his place. Balboa was not going to let another governor find *his* sea. He'd go now, he decided. Even if he didn't have a thousand men, he'd go. Gathering 180 Spaniards and 800 natives, he set out in September 1513.

As usual Leoncico, who received a captain's pay on every expedition, led the pack of attack dogs.

The trip was even harder and the going rougher than the Spaniards had expected. When they tried to wade through swamps, they found the mud so deep, they had to take off their clothes, pile them on their shields, and carry them on their heads. When they came to a river, they had to stop and build rafts. When they came to cannibals, they let loose their dogs and fired their guns, killing the chief and six hundred warriors. The rest fled for their lives. So there was nothing else to fear,

Balboa figured. If only the natives were telling the truth about that other sea.

On Sunday, September 25, the native guides pointed to a mountain ahead. From the top of that mountain, they said, the sea could be seen. Everyone scrambled up the mountain, but when they neared the top, Balboa told them to wait. What if there was no sea? He took Leoncico with him and went the rest of the way alone.

Yes! The sea was there. Blue as any sea he'd ever seen. Calling for the others to join him, he fell to his knees, praising God. Together they all sang and celebrated while the natives looked on in amazement. All this fuss about nothing more than a sea?

Four days later Balboa reached the shore, waded into the water up to his knees, and with his sword drawn, took possession of the sea (later to be called the Pacific) and all lands touching it, including, of course, China and Japan. Then he scooped up a handful of water to taste it. Yes, it was salty, but neither Balboa nor anyone else knew for sure if this was a new sea or an extension of the old one. In any case, Balboa called it the South Sea and began exploring nearby islands for pearls.

On January 19, 1514, he returned to Antigua, loaded down with large pearls and six thousand pesos' worth of gold. The settlers, wild with excitement, followed Balboa and his party in a triumphal procession. The pearls and gold were divided up: one-fifth to the king and the rest to the settlers according to their rank, some even going to Leoncico. Balboa could also be proud of the fact that he'd made friends along his route and not a single Spaniard had been lost. It was no wonder that the settlers called him a hero.

There was one outsider in town who stood by, watching the celebration. Pedro de Arbolancha had just arrived, an agent of the king sent to find out how the colony was doing and to prepare the way for a new

governor. Of course Arbolancha could see that Balboa was well liked and that the colony was doing well under him. But in case the king didn't believe it, the settlers wrote a petition, asking that Balboa be kept as their governor. If Arbolancha had hurried back to Spain with this petition, history might have been changed—at least Balboa's history. But Arbolancha hung around Antigua for three months. Perhaps he was having a good time; perhaps the weather was bad. In any case, he didn't sail for Spain until March, and by that time the new governor was already on his way to Antigua. His name was Pedrarias de Avila, but in Antigua his nickname became the Wrath of God. He arrived on June 29, 1514, with two thousand new settlers, fifty horses, one hundred cattle, eleven bells for a new church, and his brother, who became known as Count Fist-in-the Face. Worst of all, he brought back Enciso.

One of the first things de Avila did was to charge Balboa with all the offenses that he could think of. Balboa was fined and his house taken from him, but de Avila did not send him back to Spain for trial, nor did he put him in jail. Perhaps he was afraid to lock up a man who had so many friends. Perhaps he simply wanted to make use of Balboa for a while. Soon, however, it would be too late to punish him. When word reached Europe that a new sea had been discovered, Balboa became an instant hero, as popular as Columbus had been. King Ferdinand ordered de Avila "to favor and deal well with Balboa." He wrote to Balboa, praising him, calling him "Adelantado" (leader), and asking him to give advice to de Avila. But Balboa not only didn't want to give de Avila advice, de Avila didn't want to take it. Balboa complained to the king that de Avila treated the natives harshly. "Where the Indians were as sheep," he said, "they have become as fierce lions." And de Avila complained that Balboa was covetous, ungrateful, and ambitious.

But de Avila did make use of Balboa. He assigned him the job of building a road from one sea to the other with a town at each end. He was also to build ships and explore the coast that led south into the area we now call Peru. According to the natives, this was a fabulous place with so much gold, it sounded like Japan. Balboa had his heart set on this expedition, but the work proceeded so slowly that de Avila became suspicious. How could he trust Balboa? Was he already setting himself up as ruler of this new land? So de Avila sent soldiers to bring Balboa back.

On his return, Balboa was accused of treason, tried, and convicted. And in January 1519 he was beheaded. Like so many explorers, he came to a violent end. Indeed, it was said in Europe that people who thought they were going to the "new world" were more often going to the "next world." As it turned out, Francisco Pizarro, the soldier who arrested Balboa, was the one who eventually conquered Peru.

Still, the new sea was Balboa's, and hope revived that China and Japan lay only a short distance over *that* horizon.

1519 MAGELLAN'S 1522

AROUND THE WORLD VOYAGE

PACIFIC OCEAN

ATLANTIC OCEAN

INDIAN OCEAN

I I

Ferdinand Magellan

THE TROUBLE WITH BALBOA'S NEW SEA was that it was so hard to reach. And when you got there, what good was it? There were no ships waiting to take you on to Japan. It just didn't make sense: all this land and no opening to let anyone through! Columbus had tried to find a strait, and explorers continued to look and continued to fail. When Martin Waldseemüller drew his map of America, he put a strait through the isthmus that Balboa had crossed, but anyone could imagine a strait and draw it. To find one was harder. For four hundred years explorers had looked—to the north through the Arctic, to the south, up and down the eastern coasts of North and South America. Somewhere America must be connected to Asia. That's what most people thought through the sixteenth century and even into the seventeenth.

Giovanni da Verrazzano, a gentleman educated in Florence, sailing for the French king, was one of those looking for a strait. In 1524 after his latest trip, he wrote: "My intention on this voyage was to reach Cataia [China] and the extreme east coast of Asia, not expecting to find such a barrier of new land as I did find, and if I did find such a land, I estimated that it would not lack a strait to penetrate to the Eastern Ocean [Pacific]." He made a thorough search, from North Carolina down to Florida, then north all the way to Nova Scotia. And he found no strait. He did, however, think he had a glimpse of the Pacific Ocean. Sailing past the Outer Banks of North Carolina, he saw on the other side such a stretch of water, he decided it must be an ocean. (Actually, it was Pamlico Sound.) Unfortunately, he couldn't reach it. The Outer Banks was an unbroken barrier at that time with no passage through it. Besides, the water was so treacherous here, he couldn't attempt a landing. He must have hoped for an easier entry farther on.

"We sailed along the isthmus," he wrote, "in continual hope of finding some strait . . . in order to penetrate to those happy shores of Cathay [another name for China]." Some mapmakers repeated Verrazzano's mistake for centuries, showing the Pacific Ocean off North Carolina. The imaginary picture of the world was so changeable, so unsettling, that mapmakers often ignored explorers even when what they reported was correct. Many, for instance, paid no attention to Verrazzano when he concluded that the entire east coast of North America was not joined to Asia but was part of a separate world.

Ferdinand Magellan, a friend of Verrazzano's, was also interested in that elusive strait. A Portuguese, Magellan was born about 1480 and at the age of twelve became a page in the queen's household, so of course he was at the right place at the right time to hear exploring news. He may even have been present when Columbus visited the Portuguese court on his return from his first voyage in 1493. Certainly,

Magellan was caught up in the excitement surrounding Columbus. Yet what did Columbus's Indies mean to Portugal? Since his islands were in Spanish territory, Portuguese explorers would have to stick to their African route. Later, when news came that Cabral, a Portuguese, had been blown accidentally onto South American shores that turned out to be on Portugal's side of the Line of Demarcation, Ferdinand Magellan began to dream.

When Magellan finally did go to sea in 1505, he went not as an explorer, but as a common soldier on military expeditions to India by way of Africa. Just as he suspected, he fell in love with the sea and for the first time knew where he'd like to go: the Spice Islands. Up to this time the Portuguese had done their spice trading in India, but far to the west of India, between present-day Indonesia and New Guinea, lay the Spice Islands (the Moluccas), where spices were actually grown. The Portuguese reached the islands in 1511, and Francisco Serrão, a new friend Magellan had met on his travels, wrote to Magellan in Portugal.

"I have found here a new world," he said, "richer and greater than that of Vasco da Gama." Indeed, Serrão liked the islands so much, he decided to stay. He saw how happy the people were, living a lazy life in the midst of lush, tropical surroundings, and he decided to live that way too. He tried to persuade Magellan to join him, and although Magellan did dream of those islands, he was far too ambitious to want to lie under palm trees the rest of his life. He wanted to get ahead in

BORNEO

NEW GUINEA

SPICE ISLANDS

the world, and when he went to the Spice Islands, he wanted to go as an explorer and make exploring history by being the first to sail west across the new sea. First he would need the backing of a king. The trouble was that King Manuel the Fortunate did not seem to be one bit impressed by Ferdinand Magellan, even though he'd been wounded twice fighting for Portugal and deserved some consideration. Instead, the king sent Magellan to fight the Moors in North Africa. Again he was wounded, this time in his knee, which left him with a limp for the rest of his life. And now he determined he had waited long enough. He was thirty-five years old, and he would *demand* that his position be improved.

King Manuel, however, liked his subjects to entreat, not demand. When Magellan said that his pension should be increased, the king said no. When Magellan said that the king should send him to the Spice Islands as captain of a caravel, the king said no. Magellan tried to observe court etiquette by kissing the king's hand, but the king (so it was said) withdrew his hand. Magellan had one more question. Would the king mind if Magellan left Portugal to serve another monarch? King Manuel made it clear: He couldn't care less what Ferdinand Magellan did.

Magellan didn't have many friends besides Enrique, his personal slave from Malacca, a city on the Malay Peninsula just north of modern Singapore. His home couldn't be too far from the Spice Islands, because he spoke the same language. Best of all, Magellan could depend on Enrique. Indeed, he was so loyal that in his will Magellan promised that at the moment he died, Enrique would be given his freedom. Right now, in spite of being rejected by King Manuel, Magellan's fortunes were improving. Working on his dream, he studied maps in the Portuguese naval archives, talked to pilots who had sailed to the

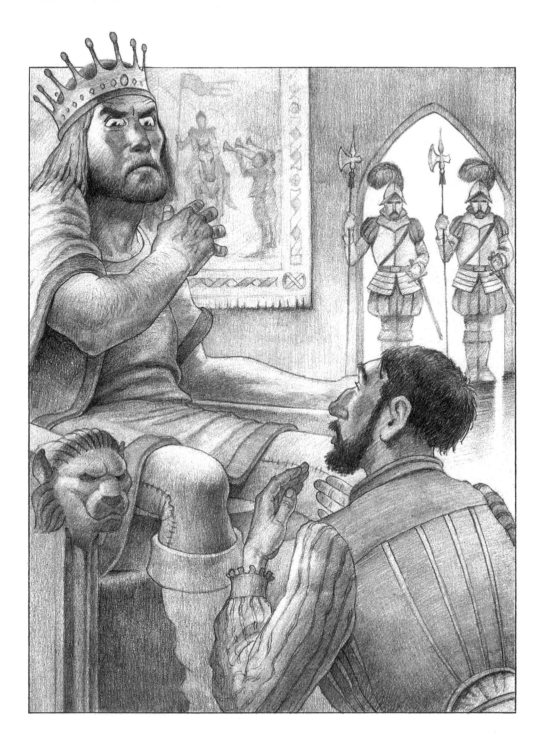

Indies, and finally confided his dream to a new friend, Ruy Faleiro, who happened to be a famous mapmaker and astronomer. Faleiro agreed that Magellan's dream was a good one. He agreed that yes, Magellan could get to the Spice Islands by sailing west. Ruy Faleiro, who had access to much secret geographic material, had heard of a strait in South America, so, of course, Magellan could sail right through to that other sea. What was more, the way Ruy figured it, the Spice Islands really fell not on the Portuguese side of the Line of Demarcation, but on the Spanish side.

Naturally, the thing to do was to go to Spain. In 1517 Magellan went to Seville to the home of Diego Barbosa, an old friend (perhaps a relative) who had long ago abandoned Portugal in favor of Spain. It was a good move for Magellan. Diego Barbosa had a daughter with whom Magellan fell in love. They were married, and all at once Magellan was a Spanish citizen with a prominent father-in-law who knew his way around court circles.

Eventually, Magellan was able to present his case to the Spanish king, Charles I. He didn't entreat and he didn't demand, but he was convincing. He persuaded the king that he had secret knowledge of a strait and he expected to sail through it and around the world, claiming the Spice Islands for Spain on the way. Magellan must have felt sure of that strait. In any case, no matter what happened, he stuck to that story. When the king asked him what he would do if he failed to find the strait, Magellan said he would just turn around and go to the Spice Islands around the Cape of Good Hope. It was such a reasonable reply, the king decided that he couldn't lose, so he promised Magellan five ships. And he agreed that once Magellan found the Spice Islands, he could keep two for himself.

On September 20, 1519, Ferdinand Magellan sailed with five ships,

265 men, the usual supply of bells and mirrors for barter, and enough food to last two years.

Magellan was naturally a secretive man who kept to himself, and he determined on his trip to communicate his plans to no one. And with good reason. The seamen were nervous enough about signing on for a two-year stint without being told that they would be sailing around the whole world. It would be like telling them that they were going to the moon. All anyone knew was that they were going through a strait to the Spice Islands. They would get rich, turn around, and go home. Not even the captains of the four other ships knew the whole story. They were Spanish noblemen who resented this ex-Portuguese newcomer, and Magellan knew that they would have to be watched. His father-in-law had warned him that there might be a mutiny. Beware of Juan de Cartagena, he said. Magellan would beware of them all. This was the first time he had been in command of men at sea, and he intended to stay in command.

Perhaps Magellan should have been more frank with his captains, for right from the first, the captains were suspicious. They had expected to sail from the Canary Islands due west on Columbus's old route, but Magellan heard that the Portuguese were waiting for him off the Canary Islands, so he ordered his ships down the coast of Africa. But of course his captains wondered why. Did he, a native of Portugal, intend to turn the ships over to the Portuguese? In the evening when the ships drew near Magellan's flagship, *Trinidad,* to receive their orders, Juan de Cartagena, the senior officer, asked about the course they were taking. Magellan snapped at Juan de Cartagena. A captain's business, he said, was to obey orders, not to ask questions.

So Juan de Cartagena didn't ask questions but he didn't forget. One evening when they were in the mid-Atlantic, clearly bound for Brazil,

Juan de Cartagena did not personally report for instructions as his ship drew up to the flagship. Instead, he had his quartermaster speak to Magellan. Obviously under Juan de Cartagena's orders, he addressed Magellan as "Captain" instead of "Captain General," his official title. When Magellan demanded that he be addressed properly, Cartagena's ship simply sailed off, and though it stayed in sight, for three days Juan de Cartagena did not report for evening instructions.

Magellan pretended to ignore this insubordination, but a few days later he called his captains to a meeting on his flagship. Juan de Cartagena came and again asked Magellan about the course they had taken. Again Magellan refused to reply and Cartagena lost his temper. Perhaps this was the excuse that Magellan was waiting for. In any case, he grabbed Juan de Cartagena by the back of his collar. "Arrest this man," he ordered.

With Juan de Cartagena confined, the fleet sailed on, arriving on December 13 in Brazil at the port we now call Rio de Janeiro. Although Brazil was Portuguese, this area was not as yet settled, so Magellan felt free to land, but, as he warned his men, they must under no circumstances harm the native people. As it turned out, there was no incentive to harm them. They were friendly, trading great quantities of pineapple, sugarcane, geese, parrots, fish, and potatoes for the worthless geegaws that the Spaniards offered. Furthermore, when the Spaniards knelt to worship, the natives knelt too, so that when he left, Magellan congratulated himself that he had converted an entire heathen community.

Magellan loved the idea of converting natives, but after thirteen days he was impatient to move down the coast to his secret strait. He found it on January 10, 1520, just where he had expected it to be—a huge bay hiding behind Cape Santa María. Everyone agreed that this was their strait. A few days more and they would be in the Spice Islands. In order

to explore the strait before actually setting his course, Magellan divided his fleet, sending the smaller vessels west and the larger ones south. For two weeks Magellan waited at the mouth of the bay for the good news that his ships would bring back. But when they returned, they had no good news. There was no strait. There was only a wide river. After going upstream, they found that the water continued to be fresh.

However disappointed Magellan felt, he did not show it. He had insisted he knew of a secret strait; he continued to insist. They would look further. So off to the south they sailed, nosing into every cove, inspecting the mouth of every river. The trouble was that it was February now, and in South America this was the beginning of winter. The farther they went, the colder it became and the more desolate. Three more bays were examined. Nothing. Still, Magellan kept on. By the end of March the men were obviously upset. They were farther south than any ship had ever been. Where was this crazy Portuguese taking them? To the South Pole? And why wouldn't he talk to them?

Magellan had several options. He could turn around and go to the Spice Islands by the African route, as he had promised the Spanish king. He could go back to Brazil to spend the winter and resume his search in the spring. He could go home. But Magellan could not give up, postpone, or turn back. Nor would he discuss the options with the other captains, the normal procedure at sea. He made up his mind alone, and on March 31, when he came to a bay with a narrow opening (Port San Julián), he led his ships in. Although it was clear almost immediately that this was not a strait either, he did not return to the coast. Instead, he ordered all five ships to drop anchor. This was where they would spend the winter. He didn't say so but his intention was obvious when he ordered everyone to go on reduced rations.

Of course Magellan knew that his decision would not be popular, and although he refused to discuss it, he thought he might smooth matters over by inviting the captains to attend Easter mass on April 1 and have breakfast with him afterward. He had the table set for five, but when the time came, the only one who showed up was his cousin, whom Magellan had made captain of the largest ship, the *San Antonio*. He must have suspected treachery, but he acted unconcerned. After all, he knew his cousin was loyal to him; and he was certain of the captain of the smallest ship, the *Santiago*, even though he hadn't come for breakfast. That made it three ships for him and two ships against him.

The mutineers had already plotted how to put Magellan at a disadvantage. Quietly at midnight thirty armed men rowed to the *San Antonio*, overcame the captain (Magellan's cousin), and put him and the other Portuguese crew members in irons. Now the mutineers were in control of three ships and Magellan could count on only two. The leaders of the mutiny were Juan de Cartagena, who had been freed, Gaspar Quesada, and Antonio Coca. None of them wanted to get in trouble when they returned to Spain, so they sent Magellan a note, giving him a chance to make peace. They had no desire to threaten him, they said, or to challenge his authority. All they asked was that he stop treating the captains like children and tell them his plans.

Magellan was not a compromising man. He captured the small boat that had brought the mutineers' message, filled the boat with armed men, seized the *Victoria*, one of the three ships held by the rebels, and sent it to the mouth of the bay, where Magellan's own ship and the *Santiago* were already in position, blocking the entrance. No one could escape. The mutiny quickly collapsed, and in accordance with his duty as commander, Magellan ordered an official trial of the three leaders. Quesada, the ringleader, was beheaded, and the other two would be put ashore and left there when the fleet sailed in the spring.

Now the men settled down to the long, gloomy winter, making daily trips ashore for firewood, repairing the ships, and hunting seabirds, which were the only sign of life in the dead landscape. But the land was not quite as dead as they thought. One day a giant tattooed man suddenly appeared, dancing and throwing sand on his white hair. Magellan recognized this as a sign of friendship, so he ordered several of his crew to prance about and throw sand on their hair. This brought more giants and giantesses out, one of whom was so tall, the Spaniards

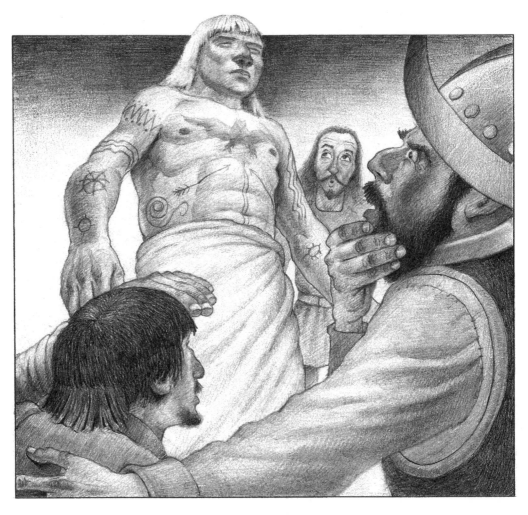

claimed they only came up to his waist. Since they also had enormous feet, Magellan called them the Patagonians, Spanish for "big-footed people." Actually, their feet were not as big as they looked. They wore an oversized skin foot-covering stuffed with straw to keep them warm.

The days dragged on, cold and endless. Finally, on October 18, 1520, Magellan gave orders to continue the search. During the winter the *Santiago* had been wrecked in a storm, so there were only four ships in the fleet now, but except for the three mutineers and one slave, all the men had survived. Moreover, they had Magellan's promise that if they did not find a strait at a certain point farther south, they would either return home or head for the Cape of Good Hope.

Two days later they came to another bay, apparently landlocked as all the rest had been except that this seemed wilder and more forbidding than the others. With its black waters and snowcapped peaks, it looked like a fiord in Norway and, as everyone knew, fiords led nowhere. There was no point in exploring it. "We all believed it was a blind alley," Antonio Pigafetta, the reporter of the expedition, wrote. But Ferdinand Magellan had not come this far to take anything for granted. He ordered two of his ships to proceed into the bay as far as they could but to return in not more than five days.

While the ships were gone a hurricane struck, so violent that those remaining with Magellan did not believe the exploring ships could have survived. When the fifth day came Magellan and the rest were ready to give up when suddenly in the distance a sail appeared. Two sails. Then a thundering bombardment. When the ships themselves hove into sight, they were flying all their flags. The men were crowded on the decks, waving, shouting.

They had found the strait! No, they had not sailed through it; they had not seen the other sea. But the water had been salty as far as they had gone; the tide rose and fell; the passage continued.

A cheer went up on all sides as the four ships proceeded through the bay. Of course no one could be sure that this was really their long-sought strait. Certainly, it was not the clear-cut, direct passage across the land that they had expected. They sailed through tortuous, twisted channels that seemed to be going nowhere. Then suddenly a bay would open up. Bay upon bay. Hidden outlets. Passageways leading to the right and left that had to be explored to determine which to follow. Still the waters remained salty; still the passage, however twisted, led west.

And at last one day two scout ships returned, firing their guns in celebration.

They had reached the other side! They had seen the other sea! Everyone must have looked at Magellan, the immovable man who never showed emotion. Ferdinand Magellan was crying. For once in his life he was overcome by his feelings. But when he pulled himself together and spoke, he showed no surprise. This was the hidden strait he'd told them about, he said. Even though the strait was 344 miles long and had taken thirty-eight days to cross, it was, Magellan said, just what he had expected.

This was the supreme moment of Magellan's life, but unfortunately bad luck was following on the heels of good luck. The *San Antonio,* the supply ship, was missing. Magellan waited and searched, thinking at first that the ship must be in trouble but eventually concluding that the *San Antonio* had secretly turned around and sailed back to Spain. The men on the remaining ships must have longed to do the same. And why not? They had found the strait. Wasn't that enough? And how could the three ships survive without their food supply? Magellan knew the risks. They would go on, he said. Even if they had to eat the leather on the ships' yards, they would go on.

So on November 28, 1520, one year and three months after leaving Spain, the three ships set sail into another unknown sea for the Spice Islands. But who could have guessed how wide this sea was? Day after day, week after week, the ships stayed in the middle of a huge blue circle that never changed and never ended. On the day they started out, Magellan had said, "May we always find [the waters] as peaceful as this morning. In this hope, I shall name this Sea of the Pacific." For this trip the sea did remain peaceful, but it was not peace that the men wanted now but land. And food. For three months and twenty days they had nothing fresh to eat and indeed little that could even be called food. Their fresh water had "gone sick," as the sailors said, and the only way they could bear the smell was to hold their noses as they drank. Their biscuits were so overrun with worms and maggots, they tried not to look as they ate. In the end they were down to sawdust and leather, and most of the men were sick. Nineteen had died.

If Magellan had only set his course ten degrees farther south, he would have found plenty of islands and would have wound up in the Spice Islands, where he wanted to be. As it was, he came to land only twice. One group of islands was so bare and lifeless, he called them the Unfortunate Islands. The other group was populated by natives who

swarmed over the ships, stealing everything in sight, even pulling nails out. Magellan named these the Thieves' Islands and sailed on as quickly as he could. On and on. Who would dream the world was so large? At last on March 16, 1521, Magellan came to what he supposed were the Spice Islands.

He was wrong. But at least the people were friendly. At least there was plenty of fresh food—bananas, coconuts, fish, oranges, vegetables, meat. He stayed nine days until his men had recovered, and then he sailed to a neighboring island, where Magellan's hopes rose. His loyal slave, Enrique, could speak to the natives! Since they had the same language, they must be close to the Spice Islands, Magellan figured. Actually, they were in what we now call the Philippine Islands, and Magellan decided that as long as he was here, he would make the people loyal to the Spanish king and turn them into Christians. He did so well on the small island of Mazzava, he thought he might as well go on to Cebu and do the same. Here he was so successful, he converted the whole island in a mass ceremony.

It was time to move on, but there was one more small island that Magellan wished to take care of before he left. The tiny island of Mactan had always been a troublemaker, feuding with Cebu, and already showing hostility to the Spaniards. Everyone warned him against it. Magellan didn't listen. This Christianizing business seemed to have gone to his head. He could not get enough of it. Besides, what was the danger? he asked. What could a group of primitive islanders do to experienced, well-armed Spaniards? Indeed, he was so sure of his strength that before he set out for Mactan on April 26, 1521, he didn't even bother to hear mass, as he always did before facing danger.

With sixty fully armed men, Magellan rowed to the shores of the island, prepared for battle but half expecting the natives to surrender peacefully. But they knew something that Magellan apparently did not know. Between Magellan's boats and the shore was a coral reef. This was low tide and the boats could not possibly cross it. From that distance even the arrows shot from their crossbows would patter harmlessly against the wooden shields the natives carried. The Spaniards would have to get out of their boats and wade ashore.

Magellan jumped into the waist-deep water and, followed by his men, went ashore, where fifteen hundred islanders were waiting with arrows, javelins, and lances. Although the rajah of Cebu had offered to provide men, Magellan had refused. They should stand on their shores and watch the Spanish victory, he said. So there they stood, waiting for the Spaniards to perform their Christian magic, but obviously they didn't have any magic. Magellan seemed all but helpless with the natives closing in on him, aiming their arrows at every part of his body that was not covered with armor. Twice they knocked his helmet off. Then they lodged a poisoned arrow in his foot. Finally, when they managed to sink a spear in his face, they rushed him, threw him headlong into the water, and killed him.

There was nothing for the survivors to do but to retreat to their ships and sail on. First, however, they wanted to collect tribute from the rajah of Cebu to take to the king of Spain. When they told Enrique, who had been acting as their interpreter, to go ashore and make arrangements, Enrique reminded them that with Magellan's death, he was now a free man. Duarte Barbosa, brother-in-law of Magellan and one of the newly elected leaders, laughed at Enrique. Once a slave, he said, always a slave. So when Enrique went ashore, he stayed ashore, abandoning his false Spanish friends. The rajah, equally disillusioned, invited twenty-nine of the Spaniards to a farewell feast. As soon as they were inside his quarters, he had them all murdered.

Of the 265 men who had left Spain, 115 survived. They struggled on in two of the three remaining ships, taking six months to reach the relatively close Spice Islands. Here they stocked up on spices which in Spain would eventually sell for ten thousand times what they paid. On December 21, 1521, the *Victoria,* the only ship considered seaworthy, set out alone with fifty men, rounding the Cape of Good Hope in the middle of May. On September 6, 1522, the *Victoria* finally limped into a Spanish harbor with eighteen haggard survivors. Fortunately, Pigafetta, the reporter who had recorded the whole incredible trip, was one of the survivors and not only could attest to the fact that Magellan's dream had been realized but could give the world a vivid description of the most treacherous exploration of all. For the first time Europeans had a sense of the whole world. They had believed that the world consisted largely of land; now they had to get used to the idea that two thirds of the world was actually water. And it was possible to sail right around it.

Ironically, the Spice Islands, such an important part of Magellan's dream, must have seemed less important to King Charles, the ruler of Spain. He sold them to Portugal for 350,000 ducats.

12

After Magellan

WAS THERE STILL AN UNKNOWN?

Of course. Even though two unknown oceans had been crossed, a new continent had been added to the world map, and islands had popped up in unexpected places, explorers continued to add bits and pieces to coastlines and continued to welcome new islands to the world. But mapmakers didn't always keep up with explorers. Sometimes a mapmaker hated to change a map that was already selling well. Sometimes they drew their maps to show the strength of their own nation in the New World. A Portuguese would emphasize Portuguese possessions; a Spaniard would concentrate on Spanish possessions. Some mapmakers had difficulty abandoning the idea of the world as Ptolemy had seen it. For a long time they started out with Ptolemy's map, revising it in minor ways as new discoveries were made, sometimes not even bothering to revise it. If a map had Ptolemy's name on it, that was enough for many people, even if they knew it was out-of-date. In any case, with the world changing as it was, it was hard to draw a satisfactory map.

Meanwhile, explorers kept on exploring. Although Magellan had found a strait that led from one ocean to the other, it was not a practical strait. It had taken him over three months to get through it and he was lucky. Many ships were wrecked trying to maneuver through a passage that was more like an obstacle course than a throughway. So explorers kept looking for another passage. When the English settled Jamestown, Virginia, John Smith nosed up Chesapeake Bay in the hope that it would open up into a strait. For hundreds of years explorer after explorer braved the Arctic waters, thinking that there might be a northwest passage. In 1903 Roald Amundsen finally did make his way across the top of the continent, but this wasn't a practical route either. Americans finally had to build themselves a strait. In 1914 a canal was completed across the Isthmus of Panama, a forty-mile-long seaway from one ocean to the other.

Maps often retained old guesses about the world that had never been proved. People still believed that there must be an undiscovered southern continent to offset all the land in the north. In many old maps this southern continent was attached to Africa, but after Bartholomew Diaz sailed around the Cape of Good Hope, that mysterious southern continent wandered about the world, sometimes taking off from the tip of South America, sometimes simply floating about the bottom of maps.

On his trip around the world (1577–80), Francis Drake discovered Tierra del Fuego at the tip of South America. Then even a bit farther south on a previously unexplored island, Henderson Island, he lay down on his stomach at its southernmost reach, stretched his arms out

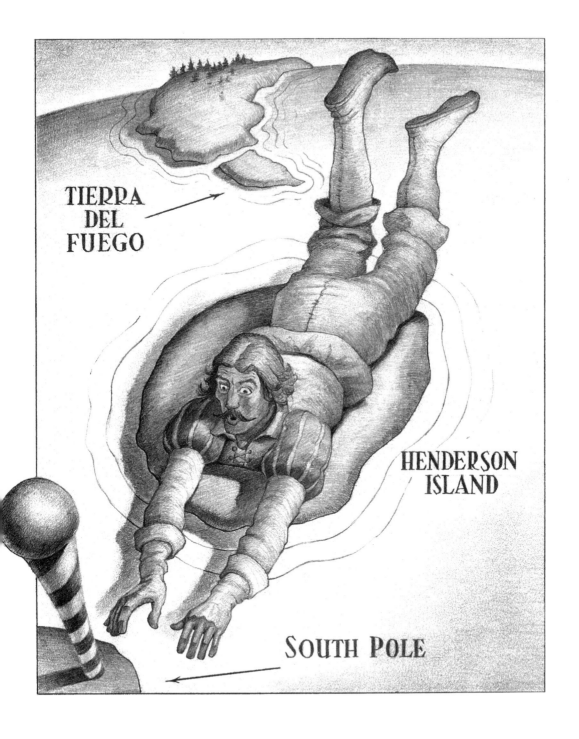

toward the South Pole, and said no one had been as far south as he had. Cape Horn was rounded for the first time in 1616. But no southern continent appeared. Still, the idea persisted.

A Dutch explorer, Abel Tasman, in 1642 sailed all the way around the continent of Australia, which Magellan's *Victoria* had narrowly missed on its way back to Spain. But his wasn't the southern continent either. It didn't extend far enough south to provide what was supposed to be the necessary equilibrium to keep the earth spinning. As late as 1767 a Scottish geographer, Alexander Dalrymple, insisted that the undiscovered southern continent was bigger than the distance from Turkey to the farthest point in China. He wanted to discover it, to be another Columbus or Magellan, but he was never given the chance.

Instead, in 1768 an Englishman, James Cook, was given a secret assignment to determine once and for all if there was a southern continent. On his first trip he sailed at forty degrees southern latitude and found nothing but mountains of ice. He went again in 1772, sailed more than 70,000 miles, and for two weeks was within the Antarctic Circle but still saw no sign of land. In the course of his explorations farther north he found the island of Tonga, the Easter Islands, and Hawaii, where he was killed by natives.

The conclusion was that there was no southern continent, which in itself was a sort of discovery. People could stop dreaming about a beautiful unknown land at the bottom of the world. Still, in 1820 an unknown coast was sighted in the south. It turned out to be the continent of Antarctica, which is still being explored.

Over the years maps have improved until now we have accurate maps that show the outline of the countries of the world as they really are. Unsuspected lands have risen from the mist; unimagined distances have been charted. Exploring has continued, as it will always continue. But the first great wave of European exploration, which began with

Henry the Navigator, took place in just a little over a hundred years. If it seems surprising that explorers could do so much in such a short time, isn't it also surprising that it took so long for explorers to get started?

Notes

Page 10 To figure out distance traveled, navigators often dropped chips of wood overboard and, using their half-hour glasses, timed how long it took the chips to go the length of the ship. Columbus, who was supposed to be a genius at "dead reckoning," as it was called, timed the chips by counting his own heartbeats.

Page 13 "The Indies" was the term people often used when they were referring to Asiatic countries.

Pages 13–15 After returning from China, Marco Polo fought with the Venetians in their continuing war with Genoa over trade in the Mediterranean. He was captured and put in prison, where he met a well-known story-writer who was interested in Marco's story. Marco dictated it to him, and that became his famous book.

Page 15 Muslims are people who follow the prophet Mohammed, just as Christians follow Jesus. At the time of the explorers they lived in parts of Arabia, Africa, and India, and had invaded or threatened to invade certain Mediterranean countries.

Page 20 Once when Prince Henry's brother asked Henry to go with him on a tour of Europe, Prince Henry declined. He wasn't interested in the known world, he said. Only the unknown one.

Page 20 Those Muslims in North Africa, the Mediterranean islands, and in southern Spain were called Moors.

Page 33 As it turned out, the store ship did not sink but made its way back to Portugal alone.

Pages 35–37 For the sake of secrecy, Diaz may have made another chart, a false one, which Columbus saw.

Page 37 In these years Portugal was on the brink of war with Spain, and Portugal's king had numerous local problems.

Page 39 The Atlantic Ocean was referred to as the Ocean Sea, part of all that unknown water that was supposed to circle the lands of the world.

Page 40 Columbus's trips down Africa were not extensive exploring ones. More likely, they were short trading trips.

Page 40 Columbus's wife had died, and when he went to Spain, he left Diego in the care of monks in a Spanish monastery.

Page 41 Many Christians, including Columbus, thought the world was due to end soon, and of course they wanted the whole world to be Christian by that time.

Page 42 Antilia, or the Antilles, were supposedly colonized by Portuguese at the time of the Moorish invasion.

Page 42 Martin Behaim's Earth Apple, which cost seventy-five dollars and took a year to make, is the oldest surviving globe. People made celestial globes of the sky before they made any of the earth.

Page 44 The *Pinta* had sailed off on its own instead of staying with the other two ships, presumably to look for gold. Columbus didn't know where it was, but on the return trip the *Pinta* rejoined Columbus.

Pages 44–45 The treaty that Spain and Portugal signed which fixed the Line of Demarcation was called the Treaty of Tordesillas.

Page 48 In addition to the slaughter, many Tainos died of illnesses introduced by Europeans. Some were so discouraged, they committed suicide.

Page 48 Not everyone was equally cruel to the natives. Bartholomew Las Casas, angry at the way the slaves were treated, spent his life trying to protect the natives and denouncing the policy of the explorers.

Page 60 Amerigo Vespucci was the first to see Brazil a few months before the Spaniard Vicente Pinzón saw it. But neither could claim the land, so Cabral, coming from Portugal and recognizing it as Portuguese territory, put it on the map.

Page 63 Because Venetians and Genoese had such control over the Red Sea, Cabot, as a Genoese, was lucky to get there.

Page 80 The story goes that when Ponce de León asked the natives what place this was, they answered, "Yucatán," which in their language meant they didn't understand.

Page 80 Cuba had been settled by colonists from Hispaniola in 1511 and would soon serve as a base for Spanish explorations.

Page 83 Since Balboa had no experience as a sailor, he probably signed on this expedition as a soldier.

Pages 84–85 Ojeda's most spectacular accomplishment had been to perform a jig on a two-hundred-foot-high plank over a street in Seville. This impressed the queen, who thought he'd prove to be a brave explorer. Nicuesa was known for being able to carve a roasted chicken in midair with his sword.

Page 86 Juan de la Cosa, who had accompanied Columbus on his second trip and had drawn the map showing Cuba as an island, was with Ojeda when he fought the natives. He too was killed.

Page 100 Ruy Faleiro became Magellan's partner, but he was so quarrelsome and difficult that Magellan relieved him of this joint command.

Pages 109–110 The Unfortunate Islands are known now as Saint Paul's Island. The Thieves' Islands are known as the Marianas.

Page 113 When *Victoria*'s men went ashore on the Cape Verde Islands, they were astounded to learn that it was Thursday onshore, not Wednesday, as it was on shipboard. They had kept a careful record of the dates, but no one realized that when you went around the world, you gained a day. For European scholars, this news was almost as exciting as the circumnavigation itself.

Bibliography

Anderson, Charles. *Life and Letters of Vasco Núñez de Balboa*. New York: Fleming H. Revell, 1941.

Ashe, Geoffrey. *Land to the West*. New York, 1962.

———. *The Quest for America*. New York: Praeger, 1971.

Beazley, C. R. *The Dawn of Modern Geography*. London, 1897–1906. Magnolia: Peter Smith.

———. *Prince Henry the Navigator*. Reprint of 1911 edition. Savage: Barnes & Noble Books, 1968.

Boorstin, Daniel. *The Discoverers*. New York: Random House, 1983.

Bradford, Ernle. *Christopher Columbus*. New York: Viking, 1973.

Brown, Lloyd A. *The Story of Maps*. New York: Bonanza Books, 1949.

Cardin, Franco. *Europe 1492*. New York: Facts on File, 1989.

Cassidy, Vincent. *The Sea Around Them*. Baton Rouge: Louisiana University Press, 1968.

Collis, John Stewart. *Christopher Columbus*. New York: Stein & Day, 1977.

Cortesao, Armando. *The Mystery of Vasco da Gama: Discovery of North America*. Lisbon, 1973.

Crone, G. R. *The Discovery of America*. New York: 1969.

Cumming, W. P.; Skelton, N. A.; and Quinn, D. B. *The Discovery of North America*. New York: American Heritage Press, 1972.

Greenblatt, Stephen. *Marvelous Possessions*. Chicago: University of Chicago Press, 1991.

Hakluyt Society. *Voyages of Christopher Columbus*, ser. LXV, vol. 1, 1929.

Harley, J. B. *Maps and the Columbian Encounter*. Milwaukee: University of Wisconsin, 1990.

Hart, Henry H. *Sea Road to the Indies*. New York: Macmillan, 1950.

Jaffe, Irma B.; Viola, Gianni Eugenio; and Rovigatti, Franca. *Imagining the New World: Columbia Iconography*. New York: Encyclopedia Italiana, 1991.

Kimble, George. *Geography in the Middle Ages*. London, 1938.

Levenson, Jay. *Circa 1492*. New Haven: Yale University Press, 1991.

MacLean, Alistair. *Captain Cook*. Garden City: Doubleday, 1972.

Morison, Samuel Eliot. *Admiral of the Ocean Sea*. Boston: Little, Brown, 1942.

————. *The European Discovery of America: The Northern Voyages*. New York: Oxford, 1971.

————. *The European Discovery of America: The Southern Voyages*. New York: Oxford, 1974.

Parry, J. H. *The Discovery of the Sea*. Berkeley: University of California Press, 1981.

Pohl, Frederick. *Amerigo Vespucci: Pilot Major*. New York: Columbia University Press, 1944.

Roditi, Edouard. *Magellan and the Pacific*. London: Faber & Faber, 1972.

Sanceau, Elaine. *Henry the Navigator*. New York: Anchor Books, 1969.

Sanderlin, George. *Across the Ocean Sea*. New York: Harper, 1966.

Skelton, R. A. *Explorers' Maps*. London, 1958.

Taylor, E. *The Haven-Finding Art*. London, 1958. New York: Elsevier, 1978.

Wilford, John Noble. *The Mapmakers*. New York: Knopf, 1981.

————. *The Mysterious History of Columbus*. New York: Knopf, 1991.

Winsor, Justin. *Narrative and Critical History of America*. Boston, 1884–89. New York: AMS Press.

Zweig, Stefan. *The Story of Magellan*. New York: Viking, 1938.

Index